The Godless Delusion

The Godless Delusion

Europe and Africa

JIM HARRIES

Foreword by Monty L. Lynn
Foreword by Stuart Ernie

WIPF & STOCK · Eugene, Oregon

THE GODLESS DELUSION
Europe and Africa

Copyright © 2017 Jim Harries. All rights reserved. Except for brief quotations in critical publications or reviews, no part of this book may be reproduced in any manner without prior written permission from the publisher. Write: Permissions, Wipf and Stock Publishers, 199 W. 8th Ave., Suite 3, Eugene, OR 97401.

Wipf & Stock
An Imprint of Wipf and Stock Publishers
199 W. 8th Ave., Suite 3
Eugene, OR 97401

www.wipfandstock.com

PAPERBACK ISBN: 978-1-5326-1498-9
HARDCOVER ISBN: 978-1-5326-1500-9
EBOOK ISBN: 978-1-5326-1499-6

Manufactured in the U.S.A.   MAY 30, 2017

Dedicated to Laura and Daniel Askew, my nephew and niece, who know me all too little due to my distant occupation that causes me to live in Africa far away from their home in England.

Contents

Foreword by Monty L. Lynn | *ix*
Foreword by Stuart Ernie | *xi*
Acknowledgments | *xiii*
Notes | *xv*
Introduction | *xix*

1   What Religion Is Not | 1
2   God In Africa | 8
3   Do We See Reality Or Do We Invent It? | 30
4   Liberal Interpretations | 47
5   Inventing Godlessness Amongst Christians | 60
6   Fortune For Atheists | 84
7   The Godly Way | 107
8   International Communication, God, and Evil | 129

Summary | *147*
Bibliography | *157*

Foreword

LINGUISTS AND ANTHROPOLOGISTS LONG have argued that culture and language do more than merely relay meaning—they set the boundaries and contours of meaning itself.

Because culture and language are intertwined, a word in one language does not necessarily connote an equivalent meaning when translated into another language. The tendrils of language twine through a cultural context, a worldview, which influences assumptions and perspectives and which accompany the word in its original context like the DNA of a cell. Even if this worldview is not visible to the speaker or listener, aspects of the cultural context continue to shape the word's meaning.

Cultural anthropologist Daniel Miller has argued that the framing effects of culture are powerful not because they are ubiquitous but because they are *invisible*—we typically don't see how our worldview is shaped by language and culture, or how language and culture shape our worldview.[1]

An increased awareness of these interconnections is possible, however, as one becomes deeply acquainted with other cultures and languages. Through comparison, our own worldviews are revealed, and the deeper one explores, the more the influence of culture and language and worldview become evident.

Jim Harries has argued observations such as these persistently in the context of western engagement in African Christian mission. In *The Godless Delusion*, Jim departs from a missions application to apply linguistic insights to a new topic—atheism. His linguistic and cultural meta-view

---

1. Miller, *Stuff*.

takes the discussion of atheism to a new level and offers fresh insights. Jim explores how the English-speaking western world culturally and linguistically frames atheism and secularism in ways that are incongruous when seen and heard through African worldviews.

Jim illustrates how English language and western secular culture define the debate about God in ways that are inconceivable in some African contexts. This comparative linguistic and cultural vantage point broadens the discussion beyond arguments to reflect the worldview embedded in western language and culture.

Jim's perspective begins by taking up western dualism which focuses debates about God on belief and unbelief and divides sacred from secular. He joins other anthropologists such as Talal Asad in undertaking an "anthropology of secularism."[2] But Jim narrows his focus to the ways in which western-originating atheism is puzzling and even inconceivable from other worldviews, betrayed by particular linguistic and cultural elements. Illustrated through African cultures and languages, Jim critiques the anthropocentric view of theology that defines God's existence by human belief. In so doing, he enables new perspectives on western debates about God.

Jim invites us to join him in traveling to other worldviews to see through different African languages and cultures. He calls for a vulnerable and patient approach to the challenging and enlightening insights that any cross-cultural journey, such as this one, portends. Jim says controversial things and the treading is deep. But he invites us into a linguistic comparison that challenges western thinking.

Perhaps most challenging is the thought that the West may have dedeveloped Africa in several ways, including in its forays of dualistic texts and discourses and its attempted export of dualistic thought. In a more hopeful turn, African perspectives might just enrich the West by holding up a linguistic and cultural mirror which teaches and deepens a mutual appreciation of the divine.

Monty L. Lynn
Abilene Christian University
Abilene, Texas USA

2. Asad, *Formations of the Secular*.

Foreword

MOST BOOKS OFFERING A critique of one kind or another involve a rearranging of the furniture. Not so with Jim Harries' book "The Godless Delusion." This book gets down to the very structure of the house itself by challenging basic assumptions about such ubiquitous and amorphous terms/ideas as "religion," "G/god," "secular," and "sacred." Harries holds nothing back in his challenge to the western view of the developing/majority world—particularly in the realms of ministry, development and aid. Even if you don't (and if you are like me, won't) agree with everything that Harries proposes, the provocation he brings is a fresh wind that wipes the slate clean, allowing us to ask ourselves: "What if we could start over? How would we conceive of and carry out this work we are called to?" And even if we don't come out the same places that Harries does, the exercise is vital! Uncovering the lingering and often unconscious biases of the Western/"Enlightened" mind, Harries reveals how, in order to live and work effectively in the Majority World (East Africa, in particular), one must be willing to meet it on its own terms—which includes an acceptance of G/god and the spiritual that is not only assumed but is viewed as synonymous with Reality and inseparable from the natural, empirical world.

Further still, Harries' message comes with and out of decades of living and working in the Majority World (East Africa); and not only living/working there but doing so in a way that is deeply shaped and effected by the very approach that he is promoting. In other words, Harries lives what he preaches. This makes his critique (sharp indeed at times) harder to dismiss and one that must be grappled with. For missionaries, development and governmental workers, or anyone interested in Western

Foreword

and Majority-World relationship this book will be deeply provoking and deeply enriching.

Stuart Ernie
Anderson University,
Anderson, Indiana USA

Acknowledgments

I AM ESPECIALLY GRATEFUL to Amy Pagarigan for providing a lot of very helpful thoughts and suggestions especially regarding the flow of ideas and arguments in this book. Some of Dr Stan Nussbaum's thoughts have also been very appreciated. I am grateful to Marilyn James for her proofreading and copyediting services. Angela Merridale helped me enormously through her typing of the original draft of the book. Many people have in diverse ways contributed to this book. I am very grateful to them all.

Notes

1. An author who tries to present an African point of view using English which presupposes categories that are NOT African, encounters several difficulties. I do basically write as a Westerner, which should make my writing comprehensible to western people. On the other hand, I also stray into more "African" territory, which could bring a little confusion to a non-astute reader. That is to say, English words are often used differently in Africa (more specifically in western Kenya where I am living) than in the UK or the USA. I will almost certainly sometimes, even if unknowingly, use words in an African way.[1]

    Western languages follow the contours of western secular contexts. This makes it hard to describe African contexts, which are all fundamentally non-secular, using English. To overcome this difficulty, I could redefine some English words so that they can be understood in a more "African" way. Such redefinition however causes its own problems: how should my reader know if subsequent use of such a "redefined" term is to be understood in the way I have redefined it, or in the original way according to standard western usage? For example, I question the clear line that the West tends to draw between God and human imagination.[2] Is the identification of God as incorporating hu-

---

1. Although I have lived in Africa since 1988, the fact that I very rarely use English in engaging with African people may mean that my English is less affected by African uses of English than that of other Westerners living in Africa. The languages I use in my day-to-day conversations with people are the Swahili and Luo languages.

2. Bloch by considering that the "transcendental social," which requires "the ability to live very largely in imagination" to be a more helpful focus for scholars than is "religion,"

Notes

man "imagination" then to be implicit in subsequent referral to him in this text, or do I subsequently continue to use the term "God" with its conventional English meanings? This question is hard to answer. The difficulty involved in answering it illustrates a problem in intercultural communication and translation. The latter has to assume that the categories of terms in another language are the same as those in "our" language. Even should I redefine a word and use it in a clearly redefined way throughout the text, it remains very likely that some readers will read only part of the book and thus miss my redefinition. They will assume that I am using conventional English. The intercultural nature of this English language text brings some unresolvable ambiguity into the English used. The same applies also to other texts, but it is not always openly acknowledged.

An alternative to redefining English words would be to use words that are not regularly used in English. For example, when referring to God in Africa I could use the term *Mungu* (a term that is widely used to translate the English term "God" for Swahili speakers). Unfortunately this practice would make the book hard to read. It would force a reader who is not familiar with Swahili to constantly keep their thumb in a glossary. This requirement may very well put off many readers.

2. Categorization of groups of people is one of the issues described under note 1 above in which I can find myself following African usage, as I understand it. The use of racially-neutral and gender-neutral terms is often preferred by western authorities, where racism can be perceived as "that terrible evil."[3] However, these kinds of terms can quickly disqualify kinds of debate that may be endemic in other parts of the world. For example, East Africans use the term *Mzungu*[4] in certain ways so as to prompt[5] certain responses by readers or hearers. In

seems to confirm my orientation to seeing human imagination as foundational to so-called religion. Bloch, "Why Religion," 2060.

3. Schirrmacher, *Racism*, 7.

4. *Mzungu* singular, *Wazungu* plural, is used to refer to Europeans and Americans, or more generally "white people." The term does not mean "white," but seems to imply that Europeans and Americans *zunguka* a great deal, i.e., tend to move around a lot. Interestingly, terms used by people in Papua New Guinea for "Whitemen" seem to have similar meanings: "those who go and come . . . moving haphazardly hither and thither . . . wanderers" Bashkow, *Meaning of Whitemen*, 5.

5. I consider words to prompt certain responses in people's minds. (See note 3 below for more detail on this on page xviii.)

order to articulate East African debate to western readers, an English term is needed to translate *Mzungu*. Common options are White, European, Westerner. If, however I use these terms in a way that is faithful to East African usage I may run into taboos in academic use of English. The same also applies to East African people's use of terms to describe themselves. A term widely used in Swahili is *Waafrica*.[6] This term is used by indigenous people in East Africa to distinguish themselves from what might be considered non-indigenous people such as Westerners, Arabs and so on. It is in my experience a widely used term that is used in certain ways to prompt certain understandings. Bringing *Waafrika* into western academic discourse as "Africans" is to enter into another arena of debate as to what may or may not be acceptable and advisable. This inevitably makes reporting from East Africa a perilous activity open to condemnation by western academics whose criterion for acceptability for use of this term is different from that found in East Africa itself. Complying with western political correctness will result in loss of foreign content, i.e., domestication of discourse [7] which could defeat the object in this book of bringing insights to the West from the non-West. My use of the terms African or Africans is, as a result of my long-term exposure to East African understandings, often in line with my perception of East African understandings of the use of *Waafrika* and *Mwafrika*, if I take Swahili as my example language. So then my use of terms like African and Westerner arises from informal oral conversational Swahili (and Luo[8]) discourse in East Africa.

It is ironic that, while the West claims to be very desirous of learning from the majority world, they want to do so very much on their own terms. Hence categories like "African" can be declared illegitimate, not because of usage or otherwise in Africa, but because of a need to fit into a western context. Such issues, I suggest in this text, contribute to there being little understanding and much misunderstanding between the West and Africa, a concern that I endeavor to address.

6. *Waafrika* could most easily be translated into English as "Africans." *Mwafrika* could be translated as "African."

7. Venuti, *Scandals of Translation*, 5.

8. I take Luo as being both the name of a language and the name of a tribe. The Luo people themselves refer to their language as *Dholuo*.

Notes

3. Amongst the linguistic innovations in this text is my understanding that words do not "mean" things. Instead, words impact, poke, prompt or prod people's minds in certain ways that result in certain reactions in their minds that in turn result in responses. This does not only apply to complex terms. "Primitives for formal analysis turn out to be higher order products of imaginative work" Fauconnier and Turner tell us.[9] I will draw extensively on Fauconnier and Turner's work. Fauconnier and Turner point out ways in which contemporary cognitive science has put the lie to notions that perception of simple objects is itself simple. Instead the subconscious imagination is much implicated. The human subconscious may work very hard indeed to present conscious understanding with inputs that seem to be simple. I will unpack this in more detail below. I point to it here to inform my reader to expect other than conventional epistemology and hermeneutics.

4. While being essentially academic, this book draws heavily from my experience of having lived in "African community" since 1988. I have lived in my current village home in one African community since 1993 while engaging in service with the church, especially Bible teaching. I include some biographical references in the text to remind the reader of this fact, and to articulate ways in which my context is affecting my understanding and communication.

    Because of parallels between Africa and other majority-world cultures, I hope the content of this text will be relevant to folks concerned with other parts of the world beyond the African continent.

5. My reader should ignore the capitalization of God in this text. I articulate the reasons for this in more detail below.

---

9. Fauconnier and Turner, *Way We Think*, 8.

Introduction

WHAT IF THE WHOLE "God delusion" approach is a neo-colonial imposition at the linguistic and philosophical level? And what if it leads to unmitigated disasters in intercultural communication and development work? As a Christian missionary working in Africa, I contend that premier intercultural communication and engagement by the West urgently needs to be placed on an overtly Christian footing. I ask "Why are there not many more western people seeking to share God's word with others in Africa, and elsewhere in the world?" I entreat my reader to give me a fair hearing. This is an academic text that is rooted in a living context. It includes some personal background and reflections.

This book is a response to Richard Dawkins' book *The God Delusion*. It is by no means a point-by-point response. Instead this book articulates arguments rooted in the practice of Christian mission work in Africa. This book suggests that development intervention, aid provision, medical programs, and numerous other interventionary strategies, if they attempt to ignore the Bible and the Christian foundation of western culture, are asking for trouble. The Christian missionary, foibles and all, is presented as the premier role model for intercultural intervention into the majority world. Continuing to deny God's role might (and certainly should) increasingly be seen as cruel perpetuation of global poverty.

As well as being a missionary, the author is also an academic. With a PhD in theology and three other degrees under his belt,[1] fifteen years

---

1. BSc Agricultural technology, MA Rural Development, MA Biblical Interpretation, all obtained in UK Universities.

Introduction

teaching Bible and theology part time at undergraduate level, some experience at supervising people for higher degrees, numerous articles and six books published, his output has already not been minor. In this book he builds on his focus on vulnerable mission to challenge what can seem to be narrow views on the side of the West about the majority world in general and Africa in particular. The term "vulnerable mission" as used in this text refers to that outreach on the part of the West to the majority world which engages using local languages and resources.

The author joins the rising crescendo of scholars who problematize the contemporary folk view of religion. According to this apparently self-evident view, religion is that which does not come under the heading of "secular," and there are many "religions" in the world. The assumption is that people outside of the West are in the process of doing what Westerners have done with "religion." That is, that they are appropriating secularism, and relegating the rest of their lives into a subordinate status of "religion." This has been found to be a grossly inaccurate portrayal of contemporary reality. It seems that outside of the West others are not doing this kind of thing. Far from it, taking other people's ways of life, like Islam and Hinduism, as "religions," is wrongly baptizing them with the identity of western Protestant Christianity. Doing such results in an interpretation of what is "foreign" as if it is domestic. It should be clear that if non-Westerners do not have "religions," then neither are they appropriating its Siamese twin, secularism.[2]

The author explores just a few of the enormous ramifications arising from the above in the intercultural context between Europe and Africa with which he is familiar. The ramifications all told are huge. They include things that he has been seeing for a long time, before he had the theoretical apparatus to explain them: for example, that witchcraft is not an excisable appendage that can simply be removed from people in Africa. So-called "African religion" is not "religion" at all in a sense of being an optional extra that can succumb to secular domination. It is core to who African people are.[3] This implies that denying God's role in African identity will increasingly be seen as a cruel perpetuation of global poverty.

Language, linguistics, and communication have long been of particular interest to the author. He has already explored translation in depth in

2. Asad, "Reading a Modern," 221.

3. See note 2 at the start of this text for the way I come to use the term "African," on page xvi.

other articles and books.[4] He continues to do the same in this account. Translation is, in many senses, plainly impossible. Very few authors seem to have paid much attention to the *direction* of translation, a key focus in this text. For effective learning, translation should be from what the author calls the "unknown" to the "known." That is, translation should be done by a member of one's own community, however defined. This is merely a continuation of the educational maxim that says that education should be from "known to unknown." If education of a community is to be from known to unknown, then as far as learning about the foreign is concerned, translation that brings it the insights that it needs must be from unknown to known. This means, for example, that the key people to inform Africa about the West "should be" Africans, and key people to inform the West about Africa "should be" Westerners.[5]

The above insight is startling in its implications. It seems to have been little considered in the literature. Educational systems around the world are modeled on, and even more critically they copy, the West. Certainly schooling in almost all of Africa is of this nature. African educational systems rely on Westerners to provide the insights, usually expressed in western languages, that their children should be acquiring. Even when Africans write materials for their own children and young people's education, they are building on a foundation erected by Westerners. Almost certainly they have to write in a way that pleases Westerners. The Westerners on whose foundations they are building are translating from their known into an unknown, the unknown being the minds of African young people. This means that African young people are having to do the impossible task of taking what is (to them) unknown, to bring their education into a known, their own lives. (The context in which western education makes sense is unknown to non-Westerners.) The implications of all this seem to be almost as radical for the West. More and more of the insights the West these days acquires about what is "foreign" are sourced from non-Westerners presenting their material to the West using English and other European languages. Some of the implications of calling this process "illegitimate" are fleshed out in the ensuing chapters in this book.

Perhaps closest to the author's heart is another major thread in this book, that which considers belief in God. Why do so many Westerners these

---

4. Many of these can be found listed here: https://wciu.academia.edu/JimHarries.

5. I have not contradicted myself here. This important notion about the directionality of translation is expounded in more detail later in this text.

xxi

days seem not to take belief in God seriously, while in Africa the Christian church is booming and seemingly central to an enormous part of people's lives? He submits that certain translation practices and confusion regarding the nature of "religion" sometimes obscure truth about God from the West. He endeavors to explain the above conundrum through unique insights gained from many decades of *vulnerable* exposure to African ways of life. The above conundrum is about language and translation, and about choice of categories. If we were to transfer some African categories to Europe, the author suggests, we would find that most (if not all) western atheists believe in God. What exactly does it mean in the first place to not believe in God? It seems to be to presuppose that the difference between the religious and the secular is a "real" difference. It is to presuppose, along with modernist philosophies already in many ways surpassed by post-modernism, that in order to be seen to "exist" God must simultaneously be unreal (God cannot simply be a part of nature) while having a foothold in the category of real.[6] That is to say, western people want to insist that for them to believe in God they need empirically verifiable evidence to convince them that he is supernatural. What is "supernatural," the author of this book suggests, is that which meets the criterion of being both real and unreal simultaneously. Yet these two invented categories are defined in such a way as to be mutually exclusive. Neither the category of real, nor the category of "non-real" are there in Africa. The author suggests that these categories are illegitimate. Western people's failure to "believe in God" is an outcome of insisting that he should fit into both these invented categories. Put aside squeezing almighty God into philosophical categories that have illegitimately been created for him, and, the author discovers, the case against belief in God is transformed.

This book is intended for a readership that can take other perspectives into account. It addresses Christian believers, atheists, secularists, missionaries, development workers and experts, anthropologists and theologians/philosophers. It challenges certain widely upheld hegemonies of the western worldview, especially the non-existence of God. It endeavors to encourage what is here referred to as "vulnerable" approaches to all kinds of development work.[7]

---

6. Although positivism has been considered by many to be largely defunct as from the 1970s, its impact on popular thinking is still very widespread. Fauconnier and Turner (*Way We Think*) enable us to see beyond positivism "to reveal the richly human nature of legal practice." (Winter, "Frame Semantics," 117.)

7. My understanding of "development work" is of course different from that of the contemporary "secular" world.

1

What Religion Is Not[1]

THE CATEGORY OF RELIGION has, in western thought, come to be taken as self-evident.[2] As English has spread globally so it appears the same notion has been spread through English beyond the West. Many people never seem to question whether the category is legitimate. As the man on the street unquestioningly assumes religion simply to be "a universal . . . phenomenon to be found anywhere in the world at any time in history," also "the scholarly world is hardly above street level" Masuzawa tells us.[3] This assumption of "a transcultural essence of religion" is "deeply problematic" according to Cavanaugh.[4] In formal circles affected by European thinking and especially by English, it seems to be assumed that "all religions are everywhere the same in essence, divergent and particular only in their ethnic,

---

1. For those unfamiliar with the school of thought that says that religion is not a legitimate category for use in the contemporary non-western world, this chapter may seem to be very brief. I do not claim to make this case here, but I refer to it. It has been made elsewhere. I summarize it in a blog that received considerable acclaim (https://www.academia.edu/16011593/Islam_Hinduism_and_Buddhism_are_NOT_religions_). I do draw on this new understanding in the rest of this book, hence I do not describe anything that is not Christianity as "religion" and I endeavor to draw on my experience of living and ministering in Africa to perceive what life actually looks like when it does not have separate secular and religious spheres. Thus I try to avoid the folly pointed to by Nongbri of trying to define what is holistic as if it is a combination of two closely integrated but still distinct sides of a dualism (Nongbri, "Dislodging").

2. Masuzawa, *Invention of World*, 2.

3. Ibid., 1.

4. Cavanaugh, *Myth of Religious Violence*, 85.

national or social expressions."[5] Contemporary scholars who question the self-evidence of this category are creating a paradox; "scholars of religion are questioning the validity of the category of religion at the very same moment when the discursive reality of religion is more widespread than ever."[6]

The classificatory system that has brought us the category known as "world religions" is really less than 100 years old.[7] According to Cavanaugh, the category of religion as we know it today did not emerge until 1700.[8] The term religion originally referred to practices of the more devoted amongst the Christian population, typically monks and nuns.[9] By contrast, those serving the church in the world were considered to be secular workers, for example priests.[10] Asad, an Islamic anthropologist, has pointed out that the contemporary category of religion has been invented by Christians, and essentially describes western Protestant Christianity.[11] Nongbri tells us "it has become clear that the isolation of something called 'religion' as a sphere of life ideally separated from politics, economics, and science is not a universal feature of human history."[12] Bloch agrees: "anthropologists have [failed to] define . . . a distinct phenomenon that can analytically be labelled 'religion.'"[13] In western people's minds, where the "norm" for the category religion seems to be modern Protestant Christianity, something is considered to be a religion in so far as it resembles or imitates modern Protestant Christianity.[14]

The effects of the above categorization on people's thinking are mind-boggling. Calling Hinduism, Buddhism and Islam "religions" has effectively given them a Christian baptism.[15] It presupposes that they have an equivalent character to that of western Protestant Christianity. Such a presupposition may be almost entirely wrong. Yet it being wrong is not preventing its

---

5. Masuzawa, *Invention of World*, 9.
6. Casanova, "Secular, Secularizations," 62.
7. Masuzawa, *Invention of World*, 22.
8. Cavanaugh, *Myth of Religious Violence*, 74.
9. Ibid., 64.
10. Ibid.
11. Asad, "Construction of Religion," 122.
12. Nongbri, *Before Religion*, 2.
13. Bloch, "Why Religion," 2055.
14. Nongbri, *Before Religion*, 18.
15. See my blog on this topic in academia.edu here: https://www.academia.edu/16011593/Islam_Hinduism_and_Buddhism_are_NOT_religions_.

being presupposed. Disciplines such as that of comparative religion have boomed and blossomed. University courses on world religions have been a winner in attracting students.[16] Upon close examination these approaches invariably domesticate non-western people's ways of life, causing them to resemble variations on modern Protestantism.[17]

A thorough realization of just how contingent and arbitrary yet widespread and hegemonic the category of religion has become implies the need for a vast immediate and far reaching game-change in the scholarly world and beyond. The West has, often unknowingly but implicitly, been categorizing "everyone else" according to a grossly incorrect presupposition regarding their resemblance with themselves. It is as if the West has been establishing its "own contingent and inevitably provincial social world as if their components were self-evident, natural, universal, and necessary."[18] The assumption that there is an identifiable category called religion which resembles western Protestantism is foundational to a vast amount of contemporary thinking.

This book looks particularly at Africa. Africans are often considered to be "religious." We must now consider this classification to be incorrect (unless they are modern western Protestants). Let me illustrate. Scholars have long identified witchcraft as having been a particular *religious* problem in Africa. The perception that religion is an optional complement to an essentially secular approach to life has contributed to African witchcraft implicitly being conceptualized as something that has somehow become wrongly attached to an otherwise rational "natural" being. If only witchcraft could be removed, the thinking goes, then we would be left with a human being cleansed of "something religious" who would as a result be sensible and logical. Hence Stepping Stones[19] activists suggest that we should "work to address the belief in child witches as it is this belief that, ultimately, leads to the abuse of innocent children."[20] This report adds: "in particular, the Akwa Ibom State Government should regulate churches, and should close any found to be carrying out child witchcraft accusations and abuse."[21] The

---

16. Masuzawa, *Invention of World*, 9–10.

17. For more on translation as a process of domestication, see Venuti, *Scandals of Translation*, 5.

18. Nongbri, "Dislodging," 455.

19. More recently entitled "Safe Child Africa."

20. Foxcroft and Secker, "Report on Accusations," 37.

21. Ibid., 37.

model has been that of secularism side-lining Christianity (i.e., religion, because only western Christianity actually deserves to be considered a "religion")[22] to make way for rationality.[23] That is, from the West's point of view, the African fear of witchcraft belonging to the category of religion has been considered to be an unnecessary vestige of some prior era that ought to be excised to leave pristine "secular man." In the course of my living and serving in Africa I have at times almost felt guilty at my realization that witchcraft fears are not an excisable vestigial organ. The implication of that realization seemed to threaten an enormous amount that the West has been presupposing. This includes very sensitive things like the West's long-held stance against racism: if witchcraft fears are not a removable vestigial organ, then that implies that Africans in Europe may be retaining something of it, and so not be *equal* to white Europeans. On the other hand, I suggest, if witchcraft fears are not a vestigial organ waiting to be excised as someone is "enlightened" with western knowledge, then perhaps witchcraft is best tackled by introducing people to faith in God (Yahweh).

The ramifications of the dissolution of the category of religion reverberate endlessly, deeply penetrating the academic status quo. It seems that much of the twentieth century's writings on the humanities will need thorough revision. It has all been written on the basis of a basic presupposition that religion is an "extra" category, therefore legitimizing the study of humans as if it were not there.[24] Now it has to be realized that such a notion is itself a religious position, an outcome of religious belief, and one that is confined largely to the Protestant West.

English itself seems to be built on the presupposition that religion is a distinct category that can somehow be quarantined into a box which allows "normal" life, engagement, communication and thinking to continue without it. If "secular" positions and disciplines such as psychiatry or psychology have to be recognized as "religious" in origin and nature, then we are stretching the English language beyond its limits. Presuppositions which relegate "religion" to a secondary category are replete with the use of terms in contemporary English such as: spiritual, science, mental health, primitive, development, witchcraft, spirits, Christian, reason, intelligence,

---

22. See also Harries, *New Foundations*, on this.

23. For Foxcroft and Secker "Child Rights" are set up to oppose "religion." See "Report on Accusations," 5.

24. Hence we have disciplines like psychiatry and anthropology that are not "religious."

imagination, evidence. We could draw a table of the English language and find that many words and concepts fit relatively neatly in one side or the other:

Religious	Sometimes ambiguous	Secular
Christianity, Islam, Faith, Spirits, Spiritual, Witchcraft, God, Eternity, Miracle, Prayer, Bible, Creator.	Awe, Imagination, Mother, Healing.	Intelligence, Science, Laughter, Emotion, Evidence, Development, Economics, House, Oxygen, Telephone, Project proposal, Psychiatry, Planets.

I will often implicitly and sometimes explicitly come back to the contents of the above table as we go forward in this book. Because the above categorizations are implicit to English, writing without presupposing them constitutes a breaking of the rules of the language. It is going outside of acceptable categories within which discussion should be confined. It is like going through the exit door out of sensible western academia into what might be perceived to be a subjective no-man's land. Although, as I have intimated above, if the groundswell recognizing the "problem" of the use of the term religion becomes a wave and then a tsunami, the whole of western academia will be required to shift and, in a sense, to start afresh.

This book is not primarily *about* the undermining of the category of religion. It does not endeavor to demonstrate that the category is not legitimate. Others have already done such spade-work. This book does begin to presuppose this category shift. This means that the contents of this book may not be appreciated by people who remain unaware of such a shift. In that sense, this book falls outside of mainstream western academics and opens new vistas. It risks condemnation by those in mainstream western academia who do not grasp what has been presented above. It blazes a new trail in anticipation that others will shortly follow. Until others begin to follow, I plead with my readers not to give me a premature write-off!

It will be hard to be consistent in language use in a new scholarship that is only just beginning to emerge.[25] I am having to guess what the new categories that will arise will actually be. I have to *abuse* existing categories. What I will be doing in a sense, is making explicit in English what is implicit in African languages. That is, making implicit translations from

---

25. I have already discussed this in my opening notes above.

African languages into English. That is, I will attempt to clearly state in English what original African languages that follow contours of indigenous thinking, in which there is no line drawn between the religious and the secular, are saying.[26]

Some point out that English is these days an African language. In a way they are of course correct; English is widely used in Africa, but this is a complex claim to make. If English is an African language, and follows African worldviews, then how does it relate to western English? Frankly, English is in eastern and southern Africa widely modelled on western (British or American) English.[27] In education and other formal circles major efforts are constantly made to keep English aligned with western standards to enable its use in communication with the West. The fact that many African people use English by imitating western usages, prevents it from becoming contextually a truly "African language."[28]

It is worth noting that in the minds of western people the category of religion has been associated with *belief in God*. As a result, changes in the popularity of "religion" have been assumed to have brought in their wake more or less faith in God. The drawing of a line between the secular and religious has over the years led some conscientious thinkers in the West to relegate the religious to some minor class, of lesser importance than the "real-thing" of the secular. Belief in God having become associated with the need for God to fall into the category of "real," while he is evidently at the same time a natural occupant of the very "unreal" that is rejected, has brought an almost unimaginable tension to European peoples. European peoples' philosophical foundations reject what they supposedly only question.[29] As a result of some of the above, some people's *belief in God* has

---

26. There may be some African languages that have found themselves following and being translations of English. Translation of such a language into English may not reveal anything particularly "African."

27. Kanyoro, "Politics of the English," 403–4, explains this situation for Kenya and Tanzania.

28. Given the prominence of English internationally, the Swahili used for government and official purposes in Tanzania is at times a mere translation from English. Ironically, this can make Tanzanian Swahili more of "follower" of English than is Kenyan Swahili. Because a higher proportion of the Kenyan population understand English than that of Tanzania, this negates the need for translation into Swahili for official purposes in Kenya. Hence one could argue that Kenyan Swahili is more of an "African language" than is Tanzanian Swahili.

29. See below for more on this internal contradiction in contemporary western ontology.

declined, such that there may have been a rise in the number of people who purport to believe in atheism.[30] Modern western atheists tend to hold that religion is of no importance to human beings. Any optionality of belief in God is very much a stranger to Africa.[31]

Finally, in this chapter, I want to mention that coming to terms with the integrated nature of the religious and the secular appears to be an essential step, if not the essential step, that will enable African and presumably more generally majority-world development.[32] But it is hard to imagine that Africans can retain such an integration while using European languages that force them into a dichotomous mode. Use of European languages enables Europeans to continue to pull African "sense" in their own directions. Hence here as in much of my other writing I advocate that the way forward for Africa ought to be (or must be) in the use of their own languages.[33]

---

30. The number of true atheists, even in Europe, still seems to be a very low figure: "Regarding atheism in Europe: The Czech Republic, where I have lived the last 18 years, is often called the most atheist country in Europe. But the careful sociological studies show that less than 5% of the population are true atheists" shared Thomas Johnson (personal communication, May 14, 2015).

31. I will look at some of the arguments presented briefly in this paragraph in more detail below.

32. As alluded to above, I here use the term development profoundly differently to the way it is used in secular circles.

33. Harries, "Glaring Gap."

2

God In Africa

SOME WESTERN PEOPLE CLAIM not to believe in God. That seems to me (and it seems to many people in Africa) to be a strange claim. It raises the question of: Who is the God whom they claim not to believe in?

It is possible to conceive of God in such a way as to render "belief in him" dubious. One can take an understanding of God, then like a straw man take it apart. If someone tells me "this pineapple is God" and I deny it, does that mean that I do not believe in God? Surely it means that I do not believe in a certain understanding about God? There is a certain perception of God that I choose not to believe in; I do not believe that God is that pineapple. To say as a result that "I do not believe in God," period, would seem to be a logical error.

There seems to be an issue here with the capitalization of the term god.[1] Christians often prefer the term God in English to be capitalized as if "God" is his personal name. That would be like suggesting that if someone says "president" when referring to Obama, the president of America, then president should be written in capitals: President. As a result, it would be correct to write that "Obama is not the president" but it would be incorrect to write that "Obama is not the President." It would be incorrect to write that "Obama is the president of America," because this should be written "the President of America." Going back to God, is to write "God does not exist" the same as writing that "god does not exist" the same as "nothing

---

1. Oral speech does not distinguish between the presence or absence of capital letters. This alone suggests that issues that arise from the capitalization or otherwise of the term god are a creation of writing practices that affect only relatively recent generations of educated people.

that could ever be called god ever existed anywhere?" What if someone is speaking rather than writing? If someone says "God does not exist," do they mean "God" or "god"? Could someone who does not believe in God still believe in god? If the capitalization of God identifies him with certain Christian conceptions of God, then someone saying they "do not believe in God" seems to mean that they "do not believe in Christianity." (Given the co-identity between Christianity and religion mentioned in chapter 1 above, does "I do not believe in God" mean that the person does not believe in "religion"?) What does it mean then to "not believe in god"? What does it mean to "not believe in Christianity"? Should we take someone's denial of Christian belief as accurate if they unquestioningly accept many implications of Christian belief that were passed down to them by their ancestors?[2] People who do "not believe in Christianity" may disagree with a certain doctrine, like the doctrine that says that the creation of the world occurred over a literal six day-and-night period. Then they are actually not "believing in" a certain interpretation of the Christian Bible. Does that really mean that they do "not believe in God"?

I would like to suggest that most, if not all, contemporary western denial of faith in God is rooted in the secular/religious dualism, and the failure to see how "religion" underlies and undergirds the very thinking that has brought about such dualism. Western denial of faith in God is a denial of the supernatural. Cassaniti and Luhrmann provide an example of the tendency to use the term "supernatural" as a synonym for God.[3] When Westerners find that the whole of life can be explained by looking at what is "natural," they question the existence of the supernatural, i.e., of God (god). Ironically, as I have mentioned in another article, non-belief in the supernatural is shared by western non-Christians and many Africans, including African Christians.[4] Thai Buddhists can also tire of talk about the "supernatural."[5] So I suggest in my above unpublished article, that in that sense either Africans (and Thais) who deny the supernatural are not religious (if we define religion as arising from belief in the supernatural), or Westerners who are atheists (i.e., who deny the supernatural) may also

---

2. For examples of aspects of western life that originated from Christianity see below, and see especially Mangalwadi, *Book That Made*.
3. Cassaniti and Luhrmann, "Encountering the Supernatural," 38.
4. Harries, "When God is Fortune."
5. Cassaniti and Luhrmann, "Encountering the Supernatural," 39.

be religious (if Africans, who deny the "existence of the supernatural," can be religious).

Rejection of God is sometimes rooted in rejection of certain understood (or perhaps misunderstood) doctrines using a logic that says that a whole faith must "hang on" one doctrine (or certain doctrines). Rejection of a certain doctrine has resulted for some in a kind of denial of a whole category of human existence, the religious, a category invented just a few hundred years ago, perhaps around 1700.[6] If belief in the supernatural is a prerequisite to being a Christian, then we might suggest also that there were no Christians prior to 1700. Going back to our capitalization of God, some people prefer to not believe God to be as Christians describe him to be. That belief-stand can then be interpreted, rather extraordinarily, as meaning that they do not believe that there is anything at all that could ever be called "god."

SOME PERSONAL BACKGROUND

Whether or not to "believe in God" seemed, at least during my upbringing in the UK, to have been a choice that one was required to make. The default choice seemed to be "no." No one seemed to question just which God was to be believed in or not believed in. On visiting our local Anglican church on one occasion together with other schoolchildren on a school outing, the boy next to me whispered about the vicar standing in front of us that "he is a woman." It was not meant as a compliment. The reason he was so described to me was because he wore gowns that appeared like a woman's dress. "Who wants to believe in a God who would make you into a woman?" I thought to myself at the time. Nothing against women, but I could see his point. The notion of "being a woman" was not attractive to me at the time (or now). Under strong peer pressure, I might at that point have denied that I "believed in God."[7] There was no doubt in my mind, as I recall, just what or who I was being encouraged to reject or to not believe in. I could also quite clearly understand why some of my friends were rejecting "belief in God."

---

6. Cavanaugh, *Myth of Religious Violence*, 159.

7. I cannot recall for certain whether I had by that time committed my life to Christ. My commitment came at the end of 1976, aged 12. Even had I made such a commitment, the notion that perhaps I ought to be associated with being a "woman" was not attractive to me.

I have picked up some of Richard Dawkins' books on occasion.[8] I have not got very far. Dawkins seems to do what I was tempted to do as a young man, to reject something that seemed to lack relevance and pertinence to the rest of life as I was experiencing it. Unlike Dawkins, I did not make the decision to "not believe in God." I thought there must be something more going on. How can it be so simple, to "not believe in God" like that, I thought to myself at the time; could god be so simple that I as a 12-year-old boy could by denying him my "belief" somehow render him irrelevant to my life? Could I make him not exist? Just who or what was I making to not exist?

I recall an occasion at a church Bible study a few years later. An old man (he may not have been very old, but he seemed old to me at the time) was sharing insights from Paul's letter to the Ephesians. I did not *get* what he said. I could hardly concentrate, so irrelevant did what he shared appear to be to my daily life. Yet he was himself clearly enthralled by what he shared. So were most of his audience, about 15 people. I was by far the youngest (I think this was in 1983). I did not "get" what he was saying, but older people did. "Who was likely to be the wisest," I asked myself, "they or I"? It seemed they ought to be wiser. Would I reject their wisdom just because I was not yet able to understand it? I decided not to do so.[9]

The decision to follow Jesus does, it seems to me, continue to have endless ramifications. These ramifications, for me at least, are far from private.[10] The implications of Christ's claims being true are phenomenal. It is difficult to imagine their being not true. The latter seems to be less often realized. It is as if many people live on the basis of vicarious beliefs. That is—on the back of the beliefs of others, be they alive or be they their ancestors. Their ancestors' beliefs set a foundation for life from which modern western people continue to benefit. In other words, a western person who decides to "not believe in God" almost certainly still lives in a way

---

8. More accurately—I have read introductory pages that are available for free over Amazon.

9. Bessenecker may think that because he encounters "pale and frail" people at missions' meetings, that we have reached the "end of world missions as we know it" (*Overturning Tables*, 20–22). Change is often good, and missions' practices will undoubtedly shift and alter. However, interest in missions being a prerogative of older folks may not mean that missions is dying. It may mean that older people are wiser, have a longer-term view and more time to give to missions' concerns.

10. Technically, it seems, in the UK, whether or not one believes in God or Jesus is considered to be a private affair.

profoundly influenced by Christianity, so deeply and profoundly has the Christian faith impacted on generations of their ancestors. Therefore, we could say that secular beliefs are founded on layers and layers of theological foundations.[11]

We are told that "God is love" (1 John 4:8). To follow God is to live a life based on love. What does a life based on love look like? I don't doubt there are many ways of living a life based on love. There is not one tapestry of love. I found a particular tapestry for myself of how, given the much poverty and suffering that there is in the world, I could live a life based on love. My approach was to decide to give my life on behalf of the poor. The question that came to me as I was engaged in making the decision on giving my life to the poor was: Is it to be all or nothing? It seemed to me it had to be all. That was my decision. It continues to be my decision to give "all." What this means to me is that, even before I set out for Africa, I had already decided that I would spend my whole life[12] in Africa (or elsewhere in the majority world) serving God in the context of poverty. If I was to be taken seriously, I had to be serious. If I was to be able to ride the storms and keep going through the buffeting waves that one meets in life, I needed direction and a clear goal. As a result, a short-term experience so common today was not an option for me.[13]

Unfortunately, a lot of uncertainty as to whether one is in the right place easily translates into a predominance of short-term mission, which results in a mission force with little local contextual knowledge. Living in Africa as a missionary, there always seem to be lots of pressures pulling one "home." Considerable determination and momentum may well be needed if one wants to stay "on the field." That momentum may well not be there if one is anyway only "trying out" one's calling and not sure in oneself that one is in the right place. Mission administrators may prefer short-term commitments that justify their saying that "then obviously God did not call you to continue" if a missionary meets certain difficulties that their bosses are unhappy with.

---

11. Berman, *Law and Revolution*, considers some of these as he reveals ways in which the modern western legal system has emerged out of the Christian church.

12. I take this as being until I am no longer able for whatever reason, which could be political, health, or retirement.

13. I have found that a missionary's worst enemy is often other missionaries. *Giriembore kendgi* a Luo colleague once said to me of missionaries. That is, with respect to missionaries, that "they chase each other away between themselves."

If I have given my all to the poor, then why am I spending this time retreating from my African village mud house to write this text to fellow Westerners? The reason is because I have found that Westerners' actions are very dominant in today's Africa. If Westerners act on the basis of ignorance, then their powerful actions can be misguided. "Over here" in Africa, Western domination over us is limiting our options. Westerners like myself who experience such domination from their own distant people first hand should, I think, take time to endeavor to educate people in the West. I am only hoping that Westerners will listen.

Talk of inappropriate domination is replete amongst Westerners, especially those exploring post-colonialism. Many such analyses that are exploring the architecture of unhealthy domination are rooted in Marxism. Frantz Fanon, described as "perhaps the pre-eminent thinker of the 20th century on the issue of decolonization"[14] who worked much on language issues,[15] leaned heavily on Karl Marx.[16] For Marx, "the history of all hitherto existing society is the history of class struggles."[17] Marx's teaching, that domination is a class phenomenon, still seems to blind contemporary scholars to ways in which the interaction of *cultures* results in unhelpful domination. It is my conviction that the contemporary orientation to countering racism, much of which could be considered a product of colonialism, acts to conceal cultural differences from view. Many authors seem to be oblivious to ways in which countering racism has become an excuse for ignoring cultural differences. Schirrmacher's text, designed to clearly lay out the nature of the issue of racism "in a nutshell," especially for the benefit of Christians in Germany and beyond, is a good example of this.[18] Schirrmacher makes great efforts to point to the fallacies associated with linking what are actually cultural traits to biology.[19] He links his determination to do so with his effort at treating all foreigners "with the same normalcy,"[20] apparently not realizing that the flip side of this is that it condemns him and his followers to not compensating for cultural differences.[21] The absence of

---

14. http://www.goodreads.com/author/show/37728.Frantz_Fanon .
15. Mazrui, "Language and the Quest."
16. Young, *Postcolonialism*, 128.
17. Marx and Engels, *Manifesto*.
18. Schirrmacher, *Racism*, 9.
19. Ibid., 12–13.
20. Ibid., 10.
21. I do not in any way "blame" Schirrmacher for this. He has written to counter

even the possibility of such compensation is, I suggest, proving extremely damaging to African and other majority world peoples today.[22] Because they are not supposed to be "different," African and other non-Western people are left with little or no room to maneuvre. Instead their educational systems, for example, are strongly modeled on the West, and often are presented in western languages such as English. Schirrmacher's book is good, for Europe, but seems not to consider wider global ramifications of the direction that he advocates. The western orientation to countering racism can give the misleading impression, as a result of its determined concealing of difference, that a short-term commitment to mission service is fully adequate.

Can one expect to be taken very seriously if all one has to offer is a token contribution of one's life?[23] If not, then short-term workers coming to "poor" countries,[24] should not expect to have "insider" experiences. For local people to attempt to enable an outsider to function and thrive in their "culture" can be a difficult and treacherous task strewn with rocks and pitfalls on the way. Half-understandings can be worse than non-understandings. If someone is committed only to a short-term, then it may be easier for their hosts to leave them ignorant than it is to try to help them to understand what is going on. Yet, being ignorant makes it hard for short-termers to make meaningful contributions. As a result, their local "value" may stretch no further than the money that they have available. For this and other reasons, foreign missionary and development workers have themselves to blame if they are in Africa often valued predominantly for their money.[25] I come across this again and again in the variety of African countries in which I find myself engaged.

---

what is to him objectionable. Many scholars do not seem to realize the possibly negative impact arising from countering racism that I point to in this book.

22. Harries, "Racism in Reverse," 183.

23. Not only does this question come to be asked of an individual. A predominance of short-termism can ironically have a "racist" impact, whereby African people are correct to assume that Westerners they meet are likely to be ignorant, because so many of them are not around long enough to be either well informed on local cultural issues or capable in local languages.

24. This unfortunately includes long-term workers who appear not to want to commit themselves for the long term. Someone who sets out to do short-term service but ends up serving over a long term often ends up having bypassed important introductory orientation experiences, such as time learning language. Failure to start right can seriously handicap them for the whole of their term of service.

25. According to the Buckwalters, describing the situation in reaching the Toba

A long-term commitment justifies investments that a short-termer probably would not consider making. One such in my case has been the commitment that I have made to rearing local children, such that I now have informally adopted orphaned African children living with me in my house.[26] The depth of relationship so enabled, I have had children with me since 1997, is hard for a short-termer to match. Furthermore, taking on children may well be unethical in the absence of an ongoing commitment. Short-term workers, or those who set out for a short term even if they end up serving for a long term, often struggle to justify investing a lot of time in learning and using local languages. This severely restricts their ability at relating.

I am moving on to some sensitive ethnic territory. Long-term exposure to a people results in learning things about them that short-termers may be unaware of, or less aware of. The faint-hearted might at this point back down. Perhaps I am a fool not to back down? I guess time will be a judge of that. The problem I am referring to is the association between African culture and skin color. Because Africa appears to have certain cultural traits different from those in the West, and residents of Africa are predominantly black, then certain cultural traits can be associated with black skin. If some of those traits are still held by the West as being "negative," one has an even more difficult situation—given especially the prominence of the West in the contemporary world. Is calling attention to those traits "racist" (implying that an identification of the traits carries the implicit suggestion that they are biological or genetic in origin) going to help to resolve issues that arise from them, or might it just occlude them from view? Should I be honest about what I find in Africa, or should I keep quiet through fear of being accused of being a racist or a neo-colonialist?

It is my conviction that, given the relative uniqueness of my position, I have a moral duty in the interests of God's works of mercy in Africa to

---

people in Argentina, but which would seem to apply equally in Africa, a missionary once complained that the people were wearing him out in their constant appeals for aid. "The missionary himself is to blame" said the Toba Indian "he came here and asked us what we needed, and we simply told him. So he just stepped into the trap." Buckwalter and Buckwalter, "Inculturation of the Gospel," 171.

26. I have been looking after orphaned children in my home since 1997. Our home languages are Luo and Swahili. I consider it my prerogative to adjust to their way of life more than they should adjust to mine. In my singleness and losing touch with my own people as I adjust to local African understandings, I sometimes feel as if I am dying every day. It is hard to know how this will all end. One day I guess I will know. Or at least if I am gone someone else will know.

endeavor to be honest to my fellow Westerners. Meeting pre-determined agendas in the West makes being honest increasingly difficult. The reasons for this are inherently sensitive and involving delicate relationships on my part. I give two examples to illustrate difficulties I face in trying to be honest to Westerners:

1. A mission organization put together a "code of conduct" to be made available to their members to assist them to form appropriate relationships with churches in different cultures. My disagreeing with the proposed code, that arose from a "debate about cultural chasms in mission," resulted in my being told by the initiator of the debate that: "I have also genuinely been trying to help . . . you . . . be part of the debate about the cultural chasm, rather than a voice on the side. It seems to me from your various responses that I have failed completely."[27] I found myself under considerable pressure, in order to become *au fait* with that organization, to accept and take on board their wisdom regarding the crossing of cultural chasms. I was under pressure to ignore acquired learning resulting from long-term field experience.

2. I am currently engaged in correspondence with a Westerner wanting to invest in some technical projects so as to help people in my vicinity of Kenya. He is putting me under pressure to advise him regarding which project is the most relevant. He seems to be oblivious to the negative implications for me, living in the local community, of having an intimate relationship with a well-to-do Westerner that can affect the way in which he might direct his funds. The possession of generous resources for distribution invariably gives someone a kind of power. Resources in Africa attract a lot of interest and incite a lot of competition.[28] For the sake of maintaining good relationships, a worker staying in an African community over a long term is wise to avoid becoming enmeshed in (sometimes corrupt) competition for resources. Becoming involved with a relative newcomer to a community who is wanting to distribute resources is particularly perilous if, as is often the case, the newcomer concerned has a very limited understanding of local ways, standards, and values. The newcomer probably knows very little about a community's valuation concerning which person

---

27. Personal details withheld, personal email to me, October 2015.

28. Maranz discusses this in some detail. Citing Ngoupande (from Central African Republic) Maranz writes that "when the cake becomes too small [as it invariably does], those dancing around it bring out their knives." Maranz, *African Friends*, 112–14.

should or should not be helped. They do not know how best to hand out resources. If the newcomer concerned is either a short-termer, or is not economically or socially dependent on the community concerned, they may themselves be relatively little affected by tensions they create as a result of the ways in which they release resources. Unfortunately, the long-term person associating with that newcomer, and being seen as affecting the way in which they allocate or use their resources, can easily find themselves implicated in the tensions that arise from the newcomer's actions. For a long-term person living in a way that is vulnerable to the local community, associating with such a newcomer risks bringing painful and arduous tensions and conflicts onto his own head. Yet one is under pressure as a long-term worker to spend more and more of one's time and energy facilitating "experiences" for short-term visitors from the West.

AFRICAN CULTURE

My experience leaves me with little doubt that black African populations have certain behavioral characteristics that from the West appear to be negative. It is also clear to me that the way out of those negatives that are truly negative is typically connected to the gospel of Jesus. Many differences I perceive between Westerners and Africans of the nature that putatively or actually "hold Africa back," are things that have changed in Europe as a result of the impact of generations of extremely committed Christianity. Mangalwadi is right: "the Bible [has] created the soul of Western civilization" (quote taken from the title of the book).[29] Appropriate transformation of African or any other culture is that which can come from deep influence of the Bible, i.e., the gospel of Jesus Christ, on people's lives. Before my reader jumps to the conclusion that I am unfairly valorizing the West, let me point out that the massive growth and life of the church in Africa seems to point to exactly the same thing. That is, African people who flock into churches in their droves week by week do so because they find something in the church that they desire and discover to be good and valuable.

As an observant Westerner, noticing cultural parallels across ethnic groups should make it evident that there are similarities even amongst people from widely dispersed parts of the African continent. For confirmation

29. Mangalwadi, *Book That Made*.

of this see Magesa,[30] and a very similar point made by Gifford.[31] That is to say, that *from a true western perspective*, African ethnicities are not as different from one another as is at times made out.[32] One aim of this text is to counter tendencies by the West to attempt to reify intra-African difference while glossing over differences between Africa and itself. The former, already mentioned in note 2 above, page xvi, arises from a reluctance to use "Africa" or "African" as a category, on the basis that use of this category would lead to too many generalizations about a very diverse group. Meanwhile, use of a western language for recognized scholarship in Africa and about Africa, and reluctance to find difference between Africa and the West through fear of being accused of being racist, results in an attempted imploding of West versus Africa differences. Gifford tells us that denominational affiliation is not the most helpful means of understanding the types of Christians found in Africa. Actually it is "(something local and cultural, something Ghanaian or African) that constitutes the really significant characteristic of all Ghana's Christians—which may also characterize other Ghanaians, even Muslims" Gifford tells us.[33] Gifford concedes that he actively "leave[s] aside much writing on African Christianity" because it "often deliberately avoids the very difference [with the West he] want[s] to address."[34]

I will attempt to expand on this a little by considering the kind of foundation for life that African tradition provides for its people. I will for this purpose focus on the traditions of the Luo people of Western Kenya. I have lived very closely to the Luo people of Kenya since 1993. I have used their language intimately almost on a daily basis since 1996.[35] The three years I spent in Zambia during which I was learning the Kaonde language (1988–1991) tell me that the Kaonde people, who live many hundreds of miles away in a very different part of the African continent have, from what ought to be a typical Westerner's point of view (leaving aside the biases

---

30. Magesa, *African Religion*, 26.

31. Gifford, *Christianity, Politics*, 8.

32. I say that this is from a "true western perspective" because a Westerner coming to Africa has to deal with both generic differences between their western way of life and the life of African people, as well as differences between the ways of life of different African communities. I am suggesting that the magnitude of the former somewhat dwarfs the latter.

33. Gifford, *Christianity, Politics*, 5.

34. Ibid., 6.

35. I learned to use Swahili in 1993, and then the Luo language in 1995.

mentioned above), much in common with the Luo of Kenya.[36] I find the same in my travels in Tanzania—I have spent many months in Tanzania engaging closely with indigenous people using the African language Swahili. My wider reading about different parts of the continent indicates the same. While of course there are differences between ethnic groups or tribes, from a Westerner's perspective similarities can be much greater than the differences.

Although English does not do justice to these things, in order to fulfil my purpose of informing the West, I feel obliged at this point to use English to attempt to illustrate my point. (This issue with English in particular, and translation in general, means that I do not claim that African people familiar with English will necessarily agree with what I state below about their people.) Luo people (and many African people) are very concerned about two things. These two things are ancestors (ghosts, spirits, demons, gods), and what is very closely and intimately related to them, witchcraft. The plural for the term for God in Swahili, i.e., *miungu,* is frequently used to refer to ancestors.[37] I take witchcraft as being very closely akin to the English category "envy."[38]

It is surely hard to imagine, and this is part of Westerners' big problem when it comes to relating to Africa, all the ramifications of living life with respect to African fear of ancestors and of envy (i.e., witchcraft). I can emphasize: belief in the efficacy of ancestors and the power of witchcraft are not people's "religion" that they hold in a creative tension with a secular "other" part of their life. Rather, the role of ancestors and the power of witchcraft is a part of people's very being. Considering African beliefs to be solely the basis of a "religion" has implicitly and misleadingly implied to the Westerner that they refer only to a certain part of life. It implies that a default secular foundation in science and nature is also sitting there somewhere waiting to be revealed whenever or if ever the "religious stuff" is brushed aside. It seems to me that this very damaging misunderstanding has misdirected endless efforts at "helping" Africa. Outside intervention

---

36. This is particularly extraordinary because it would seem that the Luo and Kaonde are historically only very distantly related. The Luo are classed as Nilotes who have migrated south from Sudan following the Nile, whereas the Kaonde are Bantu people thought to have originated in Cameroon and Nigeria in West Africa ancient history. (http://study.com/academy/lesson/ancient-west-africa-bantu-migrations-the-stateless-society.html.)

37. Healey, *Fifth Gospel,* 146.

38. Harries, "Witchcraft, Envy."

often attempts to build on this supposedly slightly hidden but otherwise universal grasp of "nature" (science, secularism). In brief, outside intervention often builds on the (false) presupposition that African people already grasp an objective functionality of the world around them. The fog that prevents them fully living according to their "grasp" of such functional objectivity are those false presuppositions considered to be their "traditional religion." Western reason, it is thought, will disperse that fog, thus revealing a pristine system of African rationality that equates to enlightened thinking in the West.[39]

Departed ancestors direct the activities of the living. The Luo, and presumably other African people, live according to numerous laws. (Although the way they categorize what the Luo refer to as their *chike*, often translated into English as "laws," may be different.) One little booklet produced to guide an old man to know how to run his home, lists 331 laws.[40] The book is written in *Dholuo*. (I have translated this book into English, but I have no copyright for my translation.[41]) I think that none of the 331 laws would, without detailed additional explanation drawing on various aspects of Luo tradition, make sense to a typical Brit or American. That is not to say that none of them are "sensible." It is to say that they cannot be correctly understood without the broader context of the nature of and details of Luo customary law. I give my translation of a few of these laws below, which I take as illustrating the general trend, by way of example.[42]

> Rule number 143. A senior wife dies, leaving a house of stone.[43] Later a child (son) of a co-wife to the senior wife lives in that house and [his

---

39. The image I have in mind here is like that of someone's removing layers of paint added over many years so as to reveal a beautiful intricate piece of art, rather like the artistry of Turkish Christian history has been exposed below the surface in the Hagia Sophia Church in Istanbul. (http://www.hagiasophia.com/160_years_old_secret.php.)

40. Raringo, *Chike Jaduong*.

41. In some ways at least, I agree that it should not be made publicly available, as translation into English so transforms the content as to radically change its character.

42. Raringo, *Chike Jaduong*, 30. This book was reprinted around 2014. The reprint has a new title, but the contents of the laws seem to be identical to the original. The new title is *Chike Nyikwa Ramogi jokanyanam* (Laws of the grandchildren of Ramogi, people of the lake, my translation). I have found copies in my local bookshop—indicating that the book is achieving a wide distribution. (Invariably almost all, if not all, the books in local bookshops are either recommended for use in primary and secondary schools, or used in churches. This book seems to be a rare exception.) There is no publisher or date given in the reprint.

43. I.e., a permanent house, rather than a house built of mud. A permanent house is

wife] gives birth to a child who then dies. Is it permissible for the husband (the child of the co-wife) to perform the necessary sexual rituals with his wife in that house, that need to be performed in order to cleanse the family of the uncleanness associated with the death of that child? ANSWER. The husband is not permitted to perform any sexual cleansing rituals in a house like that. He will have to build a temporary house in which to perform the required cleansing rituals.

Rule number 144. Is an old man permitted to eat food leftover after his son-in-law has eaten? ANSWER. The father or mother of a girl are not permitted to eat food left over after their son-in-law has eaten. It is not good for any relatives of the girl to eat such left-over food.

Rule number 145. Is a young man permitted to inherit his younger mother?[44] ANSWER. The son to a senior wife is allowed to inherit a younger wife to his father after his father's death providing that she has already had another inheritor, and that the other inheritor has been the one to build her a new house. He is not permitted to inherit a wife of his late father who is senior to his biological mother because he is not capable of cleansing the uncleanness of such a woman who has been his father's wife. In order for him to inherit a younger wife to his father her house must be on the same side of the homestead as is his. This is because he is not permitted to cross the homestead and to sleep on the opposite side.

Breaking customary law can bring calamity. This is the vein in which Raringo writes: "The sayings of the Luo tell us that a water monitor[45] sees with his eyes, and then runs. So then anyone who does not agree with the 330[46] laws in this book should wait and see with their eyes how the funerals

---

expensive to build or to replace. This raises the question of whether it should be re-used by other family members once the owner has died. In the past a house was left to fall down, or was demolished, after the death of its owner.

44. This assumes that the father is polygynous, and on his death has left a wife who is a younger wife to the boy's mother. The question is whether that boy, i.e., son, is permitted to "inherit" that younger wife. The inheritance of widows is too complex a subject for me to go into in detail here. Inheritance would involve the boy sleeping with the younger wife of his father on a regular basis at least for a period. Often the inheritor of a widow sets up a new homestead for the widow. Once he has done this the widow may push him out if she no longer wants him.

45. In the Luo language the term for water monitor sounds almost the same as the term for "sayings"; water monitor, *ng'ech*. Sayings, *ngech*.

46. Raringo here writes that there are 330 laws. The listing shows that there are 331. I

will come thick and fast." In other words: ignore these laws on pain of death! (Fear of the outcome of breaking such laws is nowadays probably less present than it once was in communities in Africa with which I am familiar because of the hold that the gospel already has on people. The gospel can transform people's take on their customary laws. God's law and God's grace can detract from fear of traditional customarily-recognized divine retribution.) There are many instances when traditional law can take precedence over what might in English be considered "kindness." For example, funeral attendance might well take precedence over care for children. Failure to attend a funeral can be considered to displease a "new" ancestor who might then bring misfortune to the family. Therefore, while a Westerner might perceive that funeral attendance by grandmothers can result in the relative neglect of orphaned grandchildren staying with them, local people are likely to consider that the magnitude of the calamity averted by attending the funeral so as to avoid displeasing the new ancestor, is greater than any misfortune that might arise from neglect of the children that results. Because of this, funeral attendance can take priority, even if children are as a result left hungry.

Contrary to the aspirations of Western visitors, African customary law does not generally bow to the pressure of western rationality.[47] This takes us back to my point above: the supposition that Africans (or anyone else outside of the Christian West for that matter) has a religion that somehow acknowledges the ascendency or even independent existence of something secular (in the way that the West understands the secular), has been a very widespread but misguided supposition. Here I am in effect saying that there is no neutral or natural rationality which the West can use as a lever or foundation from which to attack, criticize, circumvent, undermine or "correct" African traditions. Having lost that "lever" or foundation which the West has supposedly used for generations to evaluate and then try to "improve" others, we are left with a serious deficiency. At this point I believe we have no choice but to come back to theology. The closest thing the West ever had to an "objective" position from which to evaluate and assess others was actually the church and its theology.[48] The latter

---

take it that he writes 330 as an approximate number, rounding down from 331.

47. Added to the reasons for why this does not happen is the widespread practice in Africa to acquire western education in a western language. This ensures an insulation between formal education and deeply held traditional values. It helps to prevent the former from profoundly influencing the latter.

48. Notions of truth that many these days consider apply to "objectivity" clearly seem

was the fulcrum around which other debates would rage.[49] Given the fact that post-modernism (and post-structuralism, see chapter 3) is taking us back to an age without other foundations, if we are to engage successfully with majority-world countries, there is a need to accelerate the uptake of contemporary biblical and theological studies and research. In today's very multicultural world, this need raises important issues of context and power in the interpretation of the Bible and Christian tradition. I touch on these in this text. I do not here engage them at depth. I am more concerned at this stage to awaken a need than to provide answers to such issues. Until that need is clearly perceived, work done could seem to be superfluous. My role perhaps parallels that of John the Baptist, seeking to open a way (Luke 3:1–18).

I will illustrate with an example. Some colleagues were recently called to the house of a polygynist (a man with more than one wife) who had unexpectedly fallen sick. Both of his two wives were living in the same compound. The Christians who had been called to pray for the man noticed on arrival at the home that the two houses of the two wives were of unequal size. That was immediately a "danger" sign to them. On talking to people in the home, they discovered that the larger house was the one built for the second wife. Such practice is contrary to traditional law. If anyone should have a larger or better residence, then it should be the senior wife and not the junior wife. It was soon obvious to the team of Christians who had gone to pray for the man that this was the source of the problem causing his illness. Yes, they prayed, and considered their prayer to be effective; but they did not withdraw the recommendation made by the "traditional healer" who was basing his diagnosis on traditional law, that in order for the man to be cured the larger house needed to be knocked down. The Christians were ready to acknowledge that failure to knock the house down would preclude any withdrawal by the ancestors who had been angered by the infringement of their laws.

The above clearly links to witchcraft, which I have said most closely resembles "envy" in English. Co-wives have a particular name to call each other in the Luo language. A woman calls her co-wife *nyeka*. That could be translated as "my jealousy." Co-wives are renowned, evidently, for being jealous (or envious) of one another. Luo law states that the first wife must

---

to have arisen from prior understandings regarding exclusive truth claims made on behalf of Christianity.

49. And actually still is, although this is generally concealed.

have a senior status ahead of later wives. That should help to avoid ambiguity and thus hopefully witchcraft (envy).[50] Envy, I think we all appreciate, is not a physical force, but a "mystical" force. It can be a very powerful force to destruction in any society, African and European included. The way it is handled can vary between societies. The Bible discourages envy (Gal 5:19–21). It discourages undue desire for material wealth (Luke 12:13–21) and encourages contentment with one's lot (1 Tim 6:6). Some African societies seem to assume envy to be inevitable and powerful. They advocate the use of mystical forces, typically concocted by "witchdoctors," to counter people's envy (see below for more details).

In the case above of the two houses, presumably a combination of the assumed envy of the senior wife, and the consternation of ancestors whose rules had been flouted, combined to bring sickness upon the husband. Do note that the envy of the witch (i.e., in this case the senior wife) does not have to be overt for it to be effective, i.e., destructive. The senior wife may not even realize that she is a witch, but a combination of the consternation of the ancestors and the sub-conscious feelings she holds in her heart may be sufficient to have a destructive impact.[51]

Examples of the actions of spirits and witches are profoundly integrated into everyday life. As mentioned above, we need to realize that spirits and witches are not an "added extra" to "natural man" as western dualists tend to hold. We are not talking here of a false religion that clever people could carefully tease apart from the rest of their lives. Any suggestion that envy is an optional extra or vestigial organ that can be excised from people, is not a part of traditional African belief. Nongbri makes the same point for "ancient cultures."[52] "Describing ancient cultures with the rhetoric of embedded religion [as if religion is something that has become embedded into something that was already there before it and that would remain after its removal] protects us from having to do the much harder (but perhaps more necessary) task of re-imagining—outside of the framework of religion—how humans and super-humans might have interacted in the

---

50. It is not unusual for a man to be away from home for long periods. He is anyway less likely to concern himself with inter-wife issues unless he has to. Having the senior wife in charge of the homestead as a recognized legitimate position (i.e., one with which the ancestors are in agreement) can prevent a lot of difficulties.

51. In this sense Africans seem to be like the Thai people researched by Luhrmann, in that they consider the communal mind-set of a community to be enhancing or destructive to its prosperity. Cassaniti and Luhrmann, "Encountering the Supernatural," 41.

52. Nongbri, "Dislodging," 455.

ancient world."[53] "There is no simple way out of this problem," Nongbri adds.[54] As a result of its long historical isolation from the West we would expect African culture to be akin to ancient cultures. The suggestion that religion is a kind of "optional-extra" is likely to be a creation of the use of English, brought about particularly as a result of the long history of the use of English in Christian and dualistic contexts. Writing in English to a native English target audience (as this piece) about Africa, when one wants to illustrate the actions of spirits and witches, one has to point to something in a way that appears to be extraordinary. This can be misleading. It is hard to clearly communicate the very day-to-day nature, for African people, of these supposedly (to the West) "extraordinary" phenomena. As a result of the absence of dualistic thinking in Africa, descriptions of African ways of life can easily ignore the profoundly different ways in which ordinary things happen in Africa as against the way they happen in the West.

An example of an important "helpful" function of witchcraft fears would be that of preventing theft.[55] The main deterrent to theft in much of Africa is possibly the system, often known as instant justice, by which a thief (or suspected thief) can be lynched by a mob. This deterrent is certainly assisted by witchcraft fears. Because of the perceived and assumed "corruption" in African legal systems, people do not trust rational systems of achieving justice used by western-style courts. I suggest that such so-called "corruption" is inevitable where there is no objectivity.[56] (Gupta talks of ways in which the state is conceived locally in terms of a "discourse of corruption." Gupta's observations in India seem to have parallels in Africa.[57]) Instant justice is implicit to a society in which, because nature and objectivity are not there, neither is objective truth. When objective causation is absent, things still happen, but not being objective, the cause has become "mystical," which when related to human wills (whether conscious or unconscious), is equivalent to witchcraft.

Mystical forces (i.e., African gods) may not be very moral, but they are susceptible to bribery, and appreciate being fed or pampered. African men

53. Ibid.

54. Ibid., 456.

55. This issue comes up frequently in informal discussions that I have had with Kenyan, Tanzanian and Zambian people. People will use magic to in some way harm or immobilize a thief should he come to steal from them.

56. Objectivity, as known in the West, is a product of dualism.

57. Gupta, "Blurred Boundaries," 375.

(usually—probably also at times women) will often acquire, through some kind of payment which is typically animal blood, mystical forces that will help them protect their wealth. A classic story tells of a thief in a "protected" maize field being found the next morning rooted to the spot where he chose to steal, with his trousers around his ankles. The fear of being captured in such a state is sufficient to deter many a would-be thief.

I was once told that it is especially difficult to get older men (middle-aged and above) to be serious about spiritual Christianity. (I use the term "spiritual Christianity" to refer to the practices of churches with a Pentecostal leaning who engage with "evil powers" such as untoward ancestors and demons. I do not include *Roho* churches as such in this category as the latter tend to work with ancestors rather than to try to cast them out using the power of God's Holy Spirit. Neither do I include some "mission churches" who try to ignore ancestral spirits.[58]) Older men have their own homes and their own wealth (including growing crops, livestock, wives and children) for whom they are responsible. Almost invariably, older men will take out measures to prevent "attacks" on their property by the envious (i.e., by witches). Involvement in Pentecostal churches can neutralize such protective measures, thus rendering their property defenceless.

Traditional African courts would presumably have practiced something more like what we find in the Old Testament. I will give just two examples. If someone is found murdered, and the culprit is not known, then one possible course of action prescribed by the Old Testament is to break the neck of a heifer. This is presumably a way of wishing the same fate for the murderer (Deut 21:1–9). A second example, if a man suspects his wife of being unfaithful, then he can take her to the priest. The priest can force her to drink water containing dust from the tabernacle floor (Num 5:11–31). If she is guilty, Numbers 5:22 tells us that her abdomen will swell and her thigh waste away. Neither of these cases is based on a rational ascertaining of the likely guilty partner.

My reason for articulating certain aspects of life in Africa above, is so as to re-apply the same context back to our question of "do you believe in God?" The question of belief in God seems, for the typical African person, to be eminently practical. It is about what will work for them. The key issue

---

58. I here presuppose a classification of churches somewhat like that proposed by Nussbaum in 1998, unpublished, entitled "A Mission Centred Typology of African Churches." In Nussbaum's classification, we have three groups in African Christianity: classic AICs (African Indigenous Churches), Neo-Pentecostals, and Mission-founded churches.

is not about the existence or otherwise of God—"existence" as understood in the West is not even a known category, neither is there a negation of such a category. The question of whether or not God is "real" cannot be a pertinent question because in the African worldview there is no category of "real" that can be contrasted with the "unreal." It is Westerners who have divided the "real" from the "unreal" and who sometimes try to put God into the latter. Regarding the question of whether anything or everything can happen by chance is another concept invented by the West.[59] There is no *chance* in a holistic African world. The answer to the question of what makes things happen that cannot be chance is that it is that which people call god. God is there by default. He does things. He cannot but be. This means that, as far as people in Africa are concerned, any suggestion that God does not "exist" is essentially a western cultural invention, an invention that would appear to be a delusion.

Some hold that Africans are simply less intelligent than are Westerners. That view can bring a furore, but is held by some educated leaders amongst Westerners.[60] More on that is in the next section. On what basis actually does the West consider itself to have superior knowledge anyway? I suggest that any "superior" knowledge of the West has actually arisen from its relationship with God.[61] It seems strange and contradictory if the same is turned around into saying that "the existence of God is a delusion."[62]

The theology I am presenting in this chapter probably does not sound much like a traditional account of Christian theological orthodoxy. The latter parts of this chapter do not articulate that which was in my mind when my friend accused the vicar of being a woman (see above). They bring insights from Africa. I hope my reader will bear with me as we are still in the early stages of this book.

---

59. Chance, according to the 1982 Concise Oxford Dictionary is "way things happen of themselves . . . undersigned occurrence . . . absence of design or discoverable cause . . . " Outside of the West, things do not happen without cause.

60. Watson being one example: http://www.independent.co.uk/news/science/fury-at-dna-pioneers-theory-africans-are-less-intelligent-than-westerners-394898.html. So also Winther's "Burning Issue" considering the doctrine of "sameness" as surreptitiously privileging western thought (no page numbers given).

61. For more on this, see also Harries, *Secularism and Africa*, and Harries, *New Foundations*.

62. The notion that God might be a delusion has recently been popularized by Dawkins, *God Delusion*.

Someone may ask, are my accounts of African life above accurate and true? There is a good chance that someone might like to test them, by taking them to an African person to read and evaluate. While anyone is free to do that, I do not claim that my accounts above of life in Africa will necessary pass such a test. This is for at least two reasons:

1. A big issue to consider is that of translation. There are many conventions regarding how what is African should be translated into English. Some of those conventions have become widely accepted. Typically, these days the translator is an African who has learned English and not, like myself, an English man who is learning African languages and cultures. Fewer and fewer Europeans seem to be taking the long-term learning of African languages and cultures seriously. My translation as a European is bound to be rooted differently than that of an African. Simply speaking, I translate from unknown to known (from African languages that I know less well into European languages (English) that I know well). African people tend to translate from known (African languages) to (the relatively) unknown (English). On my own valuation that gives me an advantage,[63] but it also means that what I will report is different from what African people report. I can afford to tell truths that might affront Westerners, which my African colleagues may be careful to conceal.[64] Generally speaking, power interests in Africa will influence African people's translations in such a way as to render them different from mine. (For a more detailed articulation of this case of translation from unknown to known see the final chapter of this book, section 2, entitled *The need for translation to be from unknown to known*, page 136.)

2. The second reason my account may be different from an African person's account, which is related to number 1 above, is because I am

63. This seems to be a complex argument that I have not really seen addressed elsewhere in detail. It regards the legitimacy of informants. Who is best equipped to inform person A about person B given that person A is familiar with language and culture A whereas person B is familiar with language and culture B? Is the best informant a person of language and culture B who has also learned A, or is it a person of language and culture A who has also learned B? I suggest that the translator who is most legitimate is the one who translates into their own language or mother tongue. Tshehla, for one, agrees with me ("Can Anything Good," 19).

64. If Africans do not please Westerners they can be pauperized as they can be left with no income in Africa. In theory at least, if I do not please Westerners, I am returned to a country that has a buoyant social security system!

not sure that I, as translator from African languages and contexts to European languages and contexts, have really grasped what Africa is about. The tendency to read one's own understanding into someone else's actions and words is extremely pervasive. The depths of African understanding remain, I fear, largely out of sight to me. I note a comment that a Canadian White Father once shared with Joseph Healey: "I would give 20 years of my life for a thirty second bicycle ride through the mind of an African."[65] For all the exposure I have had to African ways, I sometimes still feel that I might be missing an enormous amount.

The above paragraph is my confession. I hope my reader respects me for making it. I tentatively suggest that the opposite may also be the case; that many African people have only a limited grasp of what the West is about. I appreciate that this is a more sensitive thing to say, as it implies (already mentioned above) racism. If true however, this would add to the reasons why "my explanation" may be different from "African explanations," but may not therefore be "wrong," and perhaps even should be preferred.

What should be clear to us is that God is alive and well in Africa. Although—even if not in just the way Westerners are used to thinking about God. Someone who says there is no God, in African senses of that word, may seem to be deluding themselves.

---

65. Healey, *Fifth Gospel*, 44.

3

Do We See Reality Or Do We Invent It?

DONALD HOFFMAN ASKED IN an intriguing TED talk: Do we see reality as it is?[1] The alternative to seeing reality as it is, is that actually we see invented reality. Biological evolution does not necessarily favor seeing things as they are, Hoffman tells us.[2] Hoffman gives examples where things that were apparently clear, have later been shown to be wrong. It was at one time emphatically believed that the earth was flat. Later all came to believe that it is spherical. It was once clear to everyone that the sun revolved around the earth. Later we were told that such an "obvious" explanation was incorrect, what actually happens is that the earth revolves around the sun. If something that was once so obviously true can subsequently found to be absolutely wrong, then what is next? What else do we emphatically believe that will in the future be shown to be untrue? I have looked at an example of such in chapter 1; in recent times many Westerners seem to have believed that there is something called religion, and that it is and has always existed where there are people. Now we are asked to question that "self-evident" notion. Another example: some intelligent Westerners claim that God does not exist; will people look back at the folly of such assertion?

Hoffman talks about the jewel beetle (*Buprestidae*) from Australia. For millions of years this beetle has mated very successfully, Hoffman tells us. When the male saw a particular shiny brown surface that was the back of

---

1. Hoffman, "Do We See Reality."
2. In the same light Fauconnier and Turner tell us: "Evolution seems to have built us to be constrained from looking directly into the nature of our cognition, which puts cognitive science in the difficult position of trying to use mental abilities to reveal what those very abilities are built to hide" (*Way We Think*, 34).

the female, he would alight on it and fertilize it. To the beetle that was sufficient information for effective mating. That was the perception of reality that enabled efficient reproduction. The "reality" of the fact that not all shiny brown surfaces are females did not interfere with the evolutionary progress of the jewel beetle, because there were no other similar competing shiny brown surfaces. Then the brown bottle came along. Careless Australian drinkers would simply throw their shiny brown bottles aside. To the male jewel beetle that looked just like a female. Male jewel beetles congregated on brown glass bottles. The species went into decline. Males were too busy on the bottles, leaving females unfertilized. Australian government action was needed to change the design of bottles to save the beetle! A perception of reality that had enabled the beetle to survive, according to evolutionists for millions of years or more, was clearly far from being a comprehensively true and accurate perception of reality. "Evolution does not favour . . . accurate perception of reality" Hoffman tells us. Instead, as a result of evolution "perception of reality goes extinct."[3]

Hoffman considers the nature of icons on a computer desktop. Computer users come to associate certain icons with certain things. For example, a picture of a now well-outdated square floppy disc represents a way of saving a document. A large blue W represents a text file, and so on. Icons are a further step from reality than the things they point to. There is little connection between the icons and the "real" things that they represent. Whatever connection exists is largely incidental. The value of the icons is not in their resemblance to reality. Their value lies elsewhere. Anyone who imagines that by looking closely at a blue W they will be able to read the words of a text file, is misguided. So then, given this fact in terms of computer desktops, how do we know that our perception of things on a daily basis is not of this ilk? Could it not be that "space, time and objects are not the nature of reality" at all?[4]

I don't suppose that Hoffman had intercultural perception between Africa and Europe in mind as he spoke. Yet I want to take his insights there. The West tends to see itself as having a handle on reality. That reality is taken as providing the foundation for intercultural communication. I have already mentioned that such a view presupposes a "modern" view of religion, a view that we have already seriously brought into question. Hoffman has us ask also whether the supposed realities of science are more akin to icons

3. Hoffman, "Do We See Reality."
4. Ibid.

on a computer screen than to reality itself. If neither science nor religion are "real" categories, then Westerners would need to ask themselves, on just what basis are they attempting to engage with people cross-culturally?

Fauconnier and Turner seem to anticipate some of Hoffman's conclusions.[5] They present us with a fascinating glimpse into a radical epistemology. Theirs is just one of many insights growing out of the discipline of cognitive studies that has recently expanded on the back of what can be described as the "exponential growth of computer technology."[6] On exploring possible origins of human beings' peculiar levels of intelligence by comparison with other members of the animal kingdom, Fauconnier and Turner come across what they call *blending*. What sets people apart from other creatures, they suggest, is their ability to blend. Particularly critical to them is double scope conceptual integration.[7] Humans are peculiar according to Fauconnier and Turner, that is, because of their ability at blending disparate bodies of knowledge and understanding. Their book, filled with instance after instance of such blending, shows us how amazingly simple it is for people to perform blends that completely confound the most advanced computer systems! The human mind can bring together diverse topics into one blend. The outcome is not a chaotic mix, but an extension of prior boundaries of knowledge.[8]

Scientists once assumed that an act such as recognition of a blue cup is simple. Fauconnier and Turner tell us that it is not.[9] When computer systems became more sophisticated, scientists set about "training" them to imitate the human mind in tasks such as the above. Much to their chagrin, this did not prove so straightforward. Contrary to expectations based on earlier research, apparently simple acts of human cognition were found to be incredibly complex. It transpires that previous generations of researchers who had assumed certain acts to be simple had been unaware of the subconscious activity going on in their own minds.[10] "In the case of blending, the

---

5. Fauconnier and Turner, *Way We Think*.
6. Ross and Morrison, "Measurement and Evaluation," 332.
7. Ibid., 187.
8. Gibbs tells us that "it is not clear that conceptual blending theory, despite its different conceptual and terminological perspective, is sufficiently unique to be considered the most viable psychological theory" ("Why Cognitive Linguists," 46). My use of the theory is primarily as a means of pointing to a "hidden" complexity, something which alternative theories would also be assumed to do, even if in subtly different ways.
9. Fauconnier and Turner, *Way We Think*, v.
10. Ibid., 34.

effects of the unconscious imaginative work are apprehended in consciousness, but not the operations that produce it."[11] Because all humans were capable of the same subconscious activity, certain tasks were simple for all people. Attempts at building computer models to imitate people's thinking exposed swathes of unknowns. Ironically, like Hoffman above, researchers have found that "evolution" had concealed the mind's own complexity from its users: our human minds deceive us into thinking that what we are doing is simple when actually "the way we think is not the way we think we think."[12] "Many cognitive scientists now question whether consciousness has any direct bearing on unconscious mental processes."[13] To get beyond this deception seems to require a deliberate doubting of what previously seemed obvious.

Going back to blending above, Fauconnier and Turner discovered that blending involves an incredibly complex (as far as a computer is concerned) process of putting together very different scenarios. One example they give regards a debate that was raging in the USA in the 1990s about the possibility of British Prime Minister Margaret Thatcher being president of the USA.[14] The fact that this scenario is totally unlikely did not stop it from being much discussed. That incredible notion could easily be grasped by North Americans who actively debated it, whereas computers could make no sense of it.

I bring Fauconnier and Turner into our discussion for a number of reasons. They effectively undermine many kinds of "simple" logical arguments frequently used to question the existence of God. Fauconnier and Turner tell us that human thinking just is not "simple" in that sense. This links in with my point made repeatedly in this book: that to expect to prove God's existence by seeing him impact on human thinking *from the outside* is to be erroneously dualistic and to fail to comprehend the complexity of the human mind (see page 32). Underneath apparently (to some) clear category boundaries between what is real and what is not, is a mass of hard to understand activity, actively hidden from human comprehension, going on in people's minds. That is, to say as some people do, that God being in the mind is a denial of his reality is to draw on a worldview already declared extinct by research of the likes of Fauconnier and Turner.

11. Ibid., 57.
12. Ibid., v.
13. Gibbs, "Why Cognitive Linguists," 43.
14. Fauconnier and Turner, *Way We Think*, 18–20.

Fauconnier and Turner identify themselves with Richard Dawkins.[15] They are clearly determined followers of the "theory" of evolution.[16] So determined are they to follow the lead of evolution in fact, that one could say that evolution has become their god, a thought that to me is itself intriguing. In following that line, they do make some interesting observations. Language as we know it today, according to Fauconnier and Turner, arose around 50,000 years ago.[17] It arose "quickly," i.e., there were no and are no simple language predecessors to full complex human language, because human language "is the surface manifestation of the capacity . . . [for] *double scope conceptual integration*."[18] (Emphasis in original.) Once, that is, the biological capacity had been reached, fully complex language could arise very quickly indeed.[19] Meanwhile other research based in human genetics and historical analysis of migration suggests that African people have been essentially isolated from the rest of the global human population for 50,000 plus years. This suggests that when people migrated from Africa 50,000 or more years ago,[20] they might not have had language. It is possible therefore that African people were "isolated" from others before language had developed. As a result, African people would have developed their language ability (and its links to their way of life) "from the ground up" so to speak, independently of others in other parts of the world. This intriguing possibility helps to explain the existence of a vast depth and complexity of cultural difference between black Africans from the sub-Sahara and other humans around the world.

The other major point I want to draw from Fauconnier and Turner relates more closely to blending. Fauconnier and Turner, as I have mentioned above, draw on diverse examples of the incredible human ability to double-scope blend very disparate scenarios. They make occasional mention of what we might in contemporary English term "religious issues,"

15. Ibid., 109.
16. Ibid., 34.
17. Ibid., 187.
18. Ibid., 177–179.

19. Hence Fauconnier and Turner consider language to be the great exception to the general rule in evolution that everything takes billions of years to evolve (*Way We Think*, 107). People who do not believe that evolution can occur are meanwhile, according to Fauconnier and Turner, being deceived by another blend, a misleading "God-as-designer blend," about which Dawkins very helpfully enlightens people. Fauconnier and Turner, *Way We Think*, 108.

20. https://genographic.nationalgeographic.com/human-journey/.

such as going to churches as places at which to remember the dead.[21] The massive human endeavor at blending that they seem to totally ignore is that between heaven and earth. Trying to "blend" Margaret Thatcher, Prime Minister of UK, with the American political establishment apparently resulted in many intriguing insights that could have arisen in no other way, yet that was merely an incidental passing enigma. Under Fauconnier and Turner's noses, billions of North Americans and others spend hours every Sunday plus vast efforts many days of the week, learning about and seeking to live up to a blend that transforms their lives, facilitated if you like by the church, between the Kingdom of God and current circumstances "on earth." Fauconnier and Turner's theoretical work provides us with a means of grasping such blending, that provides a basis for exploring the depths of human subconscious activity (in which it seems god might be integrally involved) referred to by them, that they totally ignore.

I would like at this point to draw on personal experience. I want to look at how Westerners perceive Africa and Africans, and compare this with their self-perception as Europeans. I suggest that when a European meets an African person he will initially presuppose similarity. That is, a European's default understanding of an African is that he or she is the same as a European.[22] This basic assumption is a source of an enormous amount of bias and partiality that subsequently can really never be overcome. The very nature of humanity means that Europeans *cannot* perceive Africans "as they are." Instead, human perception of something different or new is always on the basis of comparison with what is already familiar. Adding to that bias is the use of English, or another European language. European languages are very widely used in Africa, often for formal purposes as well as for international and intercultural communication. This means that in "formal" arenas of engagement, understanding coming from Africa to Europe is built on the foundation of European people's tradition. I want to ask just what are the implications of this kind of practice, and what might it be concealing?

Heavy borrowing from Europe can conceal a great deal. Allow me to take, just by way of example, the instance of college education. Around

---

21. Fauconnier and Turner, *Way We Think*, 316.

22. One could argue that deep innate reactions to foreignness may not suppose similarity. On the other hand, in the West one is under pressure to assume similarity to avoid being accused of racism. Difference, it seems everywhere, tends to be seen negatively. Also, it is hard to give content to "difference," at least until one has got to know the person or people concerned. For more on this, see Harries, *Communication in Mission*, 10.

Africa, many colleges have been established whose aim is to guide leaders and potential leaders of African communities. The human and physical context of these colleges can be vastly different to that of colleges in Europe. For example, perhaps a college is in a remote semi-desert region amongst cattle herders whose traditions go back into fear of witchcraft and respect for the dead. Yet, when the administration of the college become aware of the need for a written prospectus describing who they are and what they do, what will they do? Re-inventing seems hard work. Rather than starting to write their own prospectus, it is much easier to take a prospectus from a "mother" college in Europe and then adjust a few details. Doing such then results in a vastly misleading impression of resemblance to Europe. Europeans who take issue with this and argue that what goes on the ground is not what is stated in the prospectus, become victims of accusations of racism. A vast reality has, as a result of a kind of process of "transfer," been invented. Far from seeing such "invention" as bias, it is likely that once the "invention" is in place, a European who questions its rooting in reality is the one likely to be accused of showing racist partiality.[23]

The above is just one small instance forming part of a constant bombardment of resemblance to Europe that meets a western visitor to Africa. The bombardment is relentless and intense. The airline a European uses is probably co-managed by a European airline. The airport has been designed by a Westerner. The coach that picks up the visitors was once in use in Berlin. Their African host has made major efforts for twenty years to learn the European language, is used to receiving visitors from Europe, and is keen to answer questions in European ways.[24] The host knows that resemblance to Europe will impress the visitor, who is very likely to be wealthy or at least to have connections to money that can potentially flow in his direction. Resemblance to Europe can be constantly emphasized in almost every

---

23. I experienced some of these dilemmas at a theological college in Africa that I once taught at. The contradictions between what we were according to our written material and what we actually were as a result of our context were a source of great consternation to officers of an accrediting body sent to evaluate our preparedness for accreditation. The accrediting body was working on western principles, our prospectus was a carry-over from a western context; the way to get accreditation was to minimize any "troublesome" impact of African culture.

24. The educational system in Anglophone Africa almost invariably operates in English. Often the means of assessing whether or not someone is educated is their knowledge of English. A large part of the aim of education is exactly to acquire a knowledge of English. The same, according to Fanon, applies to French in Francophone Africa (*Black Skin*, 18).

interaction. The visitor may see those who have not done that, but clearly to communicate with them will have to be through a translator who will appropriately Europeanize (i.e., domesticate[25]) what is said by them.

European people have in the past excused themselves from being too concerned about the above issues, on the basis of their claim that what they have to share is interculturally valid objective truth. That is, they have presupposed the universality of the religion versus secularism divide. Hence they have assumed that anyone should, by putting aside their subjective "religious" understandings, be able to grasp the "secular"/scientific part of the message that they were communicating. They assumed that African people could separate out the scientific/objective reality of what they were communicating from "religion." On having done that, African people would be left with a space in which to put a coherent religious faith. Coherent, that is, in the sense that this "religious faith" would be confined to the "religious" sphere, unlike contemporary African "religion" that confuses (as far as Westerners are concerned) the material with the spiritual.[26] The model for that "purely religious" faith is western Protestantism. Western Protestantism is designed to make sense regardless of someone's contemporary levels of material or social prosperity. I take this quote from Reeves to explain how this should happen:

> As we know in some ways the core message of Christianity is exactly the opposite of this: Christ came not to seek fortune but to serve and to be humbled and above all to seek the lost and spend himself for them. But—and here's the ironic twist—"for this reason God highly exalted him and gave him a name which is above every other name." Phil 2:9. So Christ found his fortune by giving away his fortune first! For me this passage sets the scene for the general background principle behind all morality and, by implication, all communal living. This principle is the principle of "fortune deferment/sacrifice", a principle where we weigh one fortune against another on the basis of some kind of priority system.[27]

The new faith Africans were expected to adopt, would be one in which African Christians would no longer seek good fortune "in this world." It would resemble western Protestantism because it would run independently

25. Venuti, *Scandals of Translation*, 5.

26. For an expression of this tendency for the African to co-identify himself with his "physical" environment, see Senghor, "On Negrohood," 116–19, and elsewhere in this text.

27. Harries, "When God is Fortune," 9–10.

of the material world. Because it in this sense runs independently of the material world, it could later be put aside, as some secular Westerners claim to have put their Christian faith aside. (For more on "fortune" see chapter 6 below.)

The ability to separate out the secular/scientific part of their communication from religion, that they assumed ought to be a universal ability, gave Europeans (they thought) a foundation from which to engage interculturally. Thus they have assumed that the local people they are meeting ought, without great difficulty, to be able to appreciate what is being shared with them and then to incorporate it into their own ways of life. What however if, as Hoffman suggests, Europeans are not actually seeing *reality*? In addition, we could ask: What if even were they to be seeing reality, the latter is not what is needed for human development and advance? What if, in other words, a western perception of reality is simply unattainable without a religion that reveals it?

Post-structuralism has contributed to difficulties faced by Europeans looking for a firm basis from which to understand the wider world around them. This movement in philosophy that began in the 1960s[28] was a counter to the structuralism that through valuing "the norm"[29] "was arriving at secure knowledge."[30] I go along with some of the observations of post-structuralism, such as its stress that there are "undervalued and hidden influence[s] at work within science."[31] I would go along with post-structuralists' conviction that "the scientific determination of 'human' is always the product of extra-scientific presuppositions."[32] However, post-structuralism having contributed to a general contemporary European immunity from reality can be considered a part of the problem of what I call "kicking away the ladder." (See page 89.) Christian interpretations integrated with Greek philosophy contributed to Europeans having such secure knowledge as to be able to build a booming prosperous civilization. Now contemporary European thinking under the influence of post-structuralism can deny the existence of "reality." Those participants in the European civilization that was built on certain perceptions of "reality" who are now, as a result of conformation to post-structuralism, denying the existence of reality, and

28. Williams, *Understanding Poststructuralism*, 1.
29. Ibid., 2.
30. Ibid., 1.
31. Ibid., 16.
32. Ibid., 24.

end up unable to helpfully engage in important global issues or to guide others to reach where they are. This in an age when much of the world looks up to Europe, especially through the globalization of the European educational system. I suggest that post-structuralism in its more extreme form is premature: its foundational thinking should benefit from more recent enlightenments coming from advances in cognitive studies. I propose that what we need is: Christian post-structuralism, whereby the negative pessimism of post-structuralism is counter-balanced by the positive claims of Christian revelation.[33]

Misconceptions arising from the kinds of bias mentioned above may be enormous. How can we more accurately represent what goes on in the course of intercultural engagement? I make some suggestions below. Because of the to-date widespread strong implicit European bias, the comments below may seem to be racist.[34] My reader should note also the very contingent nature of any attempt to express a culture using a language which is vastly unrelated to that culture. I hope my reader will bear with me.

Much behavior is in Africa determined by the following of taboos. Taboos are backed by the power of ancestors; breaking of taboo is thought to result in revenge by ancestors.[35] In this sense, behavior is based on fear.[36] This includes behavior towards one's colleagues. While people-need-people in one sense, in another sense in Africa the understanding of the obligation for sociality is very different from that in Europe. An African person may much prefer to be alone, if it was not for the mutual obligation that arises

---

33. Derrida, one of the key founding figures of post-structuralism (Williams, *Understanding Poststructuralism*, 1), comes close to identifying this. For more on this see chapter 6.

34. European standards have of late been taken as the international measure to which people are expected to comply. Suggesting that people are different from that "European standard" is to risk being accused of being racist. That is to say, whether one is in Zimbabwe, Myanmar, Russia, or Washington, as far as the West is concerned the default standard that one must assume in order not to be considered racist is the same and is essentially European-White-male. This standard is these days broadcast in all kinds of globalizing media; internet, TV, etc. I hope the enormous bias implicit in such process is clear to my reader.

35. Mboya, *Richo ema*. The title of Mboya's book, *Richo ema kelo Chira*, tells us that sin (i.e., breaking of taboo) results in ancestral revenge.

36. In African languages with which I am familiar, respect and fear can be linguistically very hard to keep apart. Certainly in the Luo language the same term is used for both—so it seems to respect someone or something is to fear it/him and vice versa.

from imposed ancestral taboos.[37] Mutual obligations between people being based on fear means that they are not based on love. When examined closely, Western notions of love tend to be based on what Christ did for mankind—by giving himself as a sacrifice on the cross on behalf of sinners. That's a selfless giving of oneself for others. This applies whether or not contemporary Westerners claim to be Christian, as a result of a profound influence of Christianity over many generations.

Some readers may object to my suggestion that their understanding of "love" is so deeply influenced by Christianity. Mangalwadi illustrates this well with respect to India with his story of Sheela.[38] What might now appear to be secular common sense, originated in the Bible, Mangalwadi emphasizes.[39] I was not aware of such before coming to Africa and participating in human society that had not historically been influenced by Christianity as has the West. I think I am not alone in failing to make the above connection. An anthropologist recently came to do research in my home area of Kenya. We engaged in some conversations, and I occasionally visited her. I would like to connect two aspects of her work.[40]

1. In apparent opposition to the Millennium Development Project that this anthropologist was critiquing, she set up an alternative project which she labelled *hera*. *Hera* is the Luo language term most often translated into English as love. One day I confronted her; does she know what *hera* is? She had never considered that *hera* might not be the same as western notions of love. The possibility that this might be the case seemed to trouble her, and seemed to threaten the foundations of what she was trying to do.

---

37. This is a very difficult thing to articulate. Western people tend to like the way African people spend so much time in each other's company, and do so much together. A European made a comment to this effect to a Kenyan some years ago. "That's not my choice" was the response "the reason I do that is because I cannot afford to go it alone" (written from memory). The very person later illegally emigrated to Europe. The high divorce rate amongst blacks in North America points towards a similar issue. In traditional Africa, a woman who walks out on her husband can find herself in severe economic straits. This might mean that economics and not "love," or even the desire for relationship, might be holding marriages together. I could add many other examples that illustrate this same point, from a European point of view.

38. Mangalwadi, *Book That Made*, 60–65.

39. Ibid., 65–76.

40. She had a partner, also an American, who worked with her. For simplicity's sake, I will explain what happened as if she instigated what happened alone.

2. She also set out to use modern technology to try to get to a deep understanding of what the local people were doing. What she did, she explained to me at the time, was to loan a video camera to people, and encourage them to make a recording of that which was happening in their community which is of most importance to them. She later told me that she received hours and hours of recordings of funeral services.

The above two points come together in a book about the Luo way of life written by a Luo.[41] Chapter 20 talks about *wat*. This could be translated into English as "family" or "family relationship." "Jaluo en ng'at ma jawat ahinya" (i.e., "family relationship is very important for a Luo") emphasizes Malo.[42] A key way of expressing this importance of family relationships, that has risen in prominence since the coming of the white man to Kenya according to Malo, is the celebration of funerals.[43] I very frequently hear, in verbal discourse going on in the Luo community around me, that the premier way of showing love (i.e., *hera*) to someone, is to attend a funeral of their family member. It seems to be very clear that when the Luo speak of *hera*, which is translated into English as love, what they have in mind are kinds of behavior that demonstrate solidarity in extended-family relationships, expressed particularly in funeral attendance and investment in funerals following a death in the family.

Much of Africa does not have a long Christian history as does the West. Hence African people will understand whatever term in their language is translated into "love" differently (and of course if they use English, because of the impact of their own understandings onto English, they will understand the English term "love" differently to the way that Europeans understand it). Love, as it is known in the West, is basically absent in traditional Africa.

Agreement is of paramount importance in many African contexts. This is because actual and potential tensions arising from disagreements can result in bewitchment or the provoking of untoward ancestors. That is, if people part ways while in a state of disagreement, then either the negative feelings of the living person or the negative disposition (should they die) of the dead person, could bring harm to the one who was disagreeing. The resulting proclivity for agreement can be very confusing to the Westerners

---

41. Malo, *Jaluo*. Reading the book it becomes clear that it was written long before 1999, certainly pre-1970s.

42. Ibid., 62.

43. Ibid., 64.

who are relating to Africans. Westerners tend to value truth more than agreement. Or we could say that they prefer agreement to be on the back of "truth," whether that be scientific/secular/objective or other ideas of truth. This may not be such an important requirement in Africa, if such truth even exists or is even recognizable in the first place.

I must emphasize that the above two paragraphs are only accurate in terms of presuppositions made in Europe. That is, they are accurate in terms of native English. They are likely to be inaccurate in African Englishes, because the above differences are already built into African Englishes. For example, regarding the paragraph above on love, without a long ancestry in Christian notions of love, what people have is what they know. Because the term love is there in English, African people who use English are required to engage with it. They will give the term love its own African content. The threat implied by any suggestion that someone does not "know English" in contemporary Africa is so intense that often it must simply be refuted. (Remember as I have mentioned above, that many African people spend vast amounts of money and many decades learning English.) Telling someone that the love that they have is not love, as well as being confusing, can be enormously threatening. That will almost certainly apply even if the person actually knows that translation is always an approximate art! Furthermore, for the African, truth is a result of agreement; when people agree, truth is created. That is, when truth is that on which people agree, then agreement cannot be antagonistic to truth. Hence the paragraphs above, as also the paragraphs below, are not open to testing by "asking the African." Using African commentators to verify or otherwise what is said by Westerners about Africa has resulted in concealment of endless extant "realities," as such realities would be perceived by Europeans.[44]

Because African worldviews lack a polar distinction between material and spiritual (i.e., the religious and secular), by comparison with the West and as perceived by the West, African people are apt to see the spiritual as a source of material, and the material as a source of the spiritual. (These two categories are in much of Africa simply not considered to be distinct.) So then material things are spiritual-like, and spiritual things are material-like. This means that the spiritual is inevitably grounded in the material. There is no "pure spiritual," there is no "pure material." This mixture or particular combination of categories can cause great consternation in engagement

---

44. For more on this see the final chapter of this book, section 2, entitled *The need for translation to be from unknown to known*, page 136.

with Westerners. The prosperity gospel is one of its clear outcomes—it is very hard (or more accurately let us say it is impossible), for many African people to appreciate the value of a gospel message that does not at the same time bring material gain. It is hard (impossible?) for these Africans to imagine achieving physical success without first having made appropriate provision in the spiritual sphere. My language use here continues to be European, because African people themselves do not distinguish these two spheres! For the sake of my readers, who I assume to be western, I am using European categories where they do not apply. Thus I am falling into the trap mentioned by Nongbri of "presenting back to [Europeans] the taxonomies that help to establish [their] . . . own contingent and inevitably provincial social world as if their components were self-evident, natural, universal, and necessary."[45] I am forced to do this in order to attempt to communicate clearly to Europeans using English.

The dominance and presumed efficacy of ancestors is such that it is hard, at least in many African churches, to imagine a preached message that does not in some way draw on ancestral power. The way ancestors become involved may be hard for Westerners to discern. The Bible itself talks of angels, spirits and especially the Holy Spirit. These in Africa become popular euphemisms for "ancestors." By way of example, on the day that I am writing this, I listened to a message by an African preacher that emphasized the importance of tithing. In addition to the exaltation we were given to tithe, came also an admonition that those who failed to tithe would lose out on blessings of the "Holy Spirit." Ancestors who traditionally stand behind African customary law codes here began backing biblical law. Another way of saying this would be: that in Africa, biblical angels/spirits easily take the character of African ancestors.

My experience is particularly amongst the Luo tribe in Kenya, whose language I know well. Just to talk about the Luo would however be failing to realize that African ways of life and tradition resemble one another. This is one reason why I make much reference to "Africans" as a whole, i.e., on the assumption that they have a lot in common. I suspect that other African ethnic groups have something similar to what is by the Kenya Luo people called *chira*.[46] Fear of *chira* can seriously dominate Luo people's

45. Nongbri, "Dislodging," 455.

46. My reader may want to dispute this assumption of similarity between different African ethnicities. Thus is, as I have already mentioned above, much ink spilt on trying to prove similarities between African and European peoples to avoid accusations of racism. I am disputing such clear partiality in Westerners' evaluations of "the other." Seeing

(African people's) ways of life. *Chira* is a kind of curse; it is misfortune writ large. *Chira* is considered to arise as a result of breaking ancestral prescription. Classic symptoms of *chira* are very much like those of AIDS: wasting, growing thin and weak, eventually death. Hence *chira* and AIDS are often conflated in the understanding of Luo people.

Finally, I offer another point concerning terminology. Perhaps the most widely used Swahili term for God is *Mungu*.[47] The plural of *Mungu* which is *Miungu* is often used to refer to what we could in English call "ancestral spirits." Going back to Dawkins' suggestion that God is a delusion, it seems that God and gods have an essential role to play in many, if not all, African ways of life. I don't think that is what Dawkins had in mind when he talked of delusion. What Dawkins is really saying is that God is not in the "real" category, in which case to him he belongs in the "delusion" or "non-real" category. Ironically, it may be only western people profoundly influenced by Christianity who can take God as being a delusion, because it is only they who live by the spiritual versus "real" divide on which the very term "delusion" is based. It is strange that faith in the Christian God (which has for centuries shaped the English that Dawkins is using) would seem to be a necessary prior step to concluding that God is a delusion. Is the God who Dawkins thinks is a delusion really such, if his impact on human thinking has included the invention of the very term that is now being used to describe him?

Although I have taken Hoffman's talk somewhat beyond the vision that he probably imagined for it, I think we still have a good enough fit to his main idea. Hoffman asks "do we see reality as it is?" If "we" (i.e., this presumably refers to Hoffman's fellow (liberal?—see the next chapter) Americans) do so, the implication is that we have a lot of work to do to train others also to see it *correctly*. Yet Hoffman's doubts regarding our perception of reality I think are very well placed: even traditional Westerners[48]

African people having a resemblance that is other than European requires some humility by Westerners.

47. There is an added complication here with the use of *Mungu* as a translation for God that I can mention in passing. According to Swahili noun classes, *Mungu* falls into a class of non-living things. Hence there is an implicit linguistic implication that *Mungu* is not of the nature of a "living thing," but by implication more of a "force." This kind of thing could make Swahili theology very interesting to engage. For parallel concerns with reference to the related Sesotho language of South Africa see Tshehla, "Can Anything Good," 19–20.

48. I.e., those not subsumed under post-structuralism, see above, who perhaps fail to see the reality that their forefathers saw.

are not perceiving objective reality as it is. They perceive an invented version of reality. In the terms we are outlining in this book, that is a version of reality revealed to them by particular god(s). Let us compare this to a driver arriving at a previously unknown road junction. At this junction there are hundreds of alternative exits. From the position of the junction, there is no clear indication as to where the different roads are leading. Yet the driver knows that only one of the roads will take him where he should be going. Technically modern man says that the driver takes the correct road by chance. According to the theory of evolution, drivers who follow alternative routes end up becoming extinct. We are suggesting that history tells us that the hint as to which route to follow comes from God.

As I mention in discussion above, Fauconnier and Turner get very close to realizing the impact of God on people, but they for some reason choose to ignore nearly all of the undeniably massive impact on human society that "blending" between God(s) and people has had.[49] The reason they choose to ignore this is presumably because they are following a "god" of secularism, whose reality we brought into question in the first chapter of this book.

Fifty thousand is only 0.005% of just one billion. Something seems to have taken over from chance to allow all the developments that have occurred in the last 50,000 years. Incredible changes have occurred much more recently in the "modern era," that extends for maybe the last 500 years, that is 0.00005% of one billion. The "something" is god.[50]

It follows from the above that western people's version of reality cannot legitimately claim universality on other than a theological basis. It is wrong to suppose that western versions of reality were arrived at through objective research. That is not to say that because it is not reality "as such" (i.e., reality as discovered through reality) their version of reality is not useful or valuable, but it is to say that there is no rational course of understanding that someone needs to follow in order to discover it. (In absolute terms, rationally speaking, it is arbitrary.) Because they cannot perceive reality "as it is," people need god(s) to direct them to make choices that in turn determine their views of reality. Christianity has provided the theology that has shaped western views of reality. That has in turn unearthed

---

49. They do not ignore the apparently negative effect that a God-blend has had on people's faith in evolution (Fauconnier and Turner, *Way We Think*, 108) causing people to forget the sheer magnitude of "billions of years."

50. I.e., perhaps a part of God/god or his actions.

things like science which have transformed modern life. I propose that to share the gospel of Jesus is to share the beginnings of access to "reality" as Westerners perceive it. That version of reality is "truth" in so far as it is God-ordained. It enables engagement with some kinds of objectivity, but it does not originate in objectivity. Because "development" is related to objectivity, much western development has arisen through application of scientific and technical knowledge, so development has been enabled through theology. To share the gospel is to share foundations that contribute to sustainable development. It is to share the fundamentals of what *development* and the associated human justice ought to be actually all about.

4

Liberal Interpretations

SCHOLARS CONSIDER ISSUES AT depth. Non-academics frequently rely on them for their insights. Scholars seek to set many of the foundations on which others build understanding for their lives. People expect them to know what they are talking about. They have a key role. What, then, is the basis for their work?

The notion that open debate results in "truth" is, according to Asad, a Christian one.[1] It is deeply ingrained in many Westerners today. To myself as someone raised in the UK, it seems to be a foundational truth that is beyond question or doubt. It seems this is not so for everyone. Some may have more faith in "words from the gods" than in human deliberations. Hence Blunt points out with respect to Kenya that many people seem to have more faith in prophets than in the words of human authorities: "since the senses can no longer determine the 'true' nature of things or people, Pentecostals must rely on the Holy Spirit for their insight."[2]

There are many good reasons for not believing what people say. Most would add: particularly politicians! Try as one might—truth can be slippery. Bias is constant. So is the presence of numerous interests, never mind interpretations. Interpretations are influenced by interests of all kinds,

---

1. Asad, "Freedom of Speech," 287.

2. Blunt, "Satan Is An Imitator," 318; see also 325. Blunt is typical of western authors in his assumption that there is an objective "normal" way of understanding that has in Kenya recently been corrupted. Hence he tells us that Kenyan people's senses "can no longer" determine truth, as if at one time they could do so. Blunt implicitly but incorrectly assumes, as we see does much western scholarship, that a truly (western) secular part of people's lives exists but has been "corrupted" by "religion."

some of those are incentive based—for example a desire to boost one's income. Some may be fear based—avoiding what could spoil future opportunities. There are half-truths. There are lies. There are ruses designed to deflect attention. Matters can be given a certain spin. Interpretations can be dictated by the way an analysis is framed.[3,4] Different communities use the same language differently, sometimes vastly differently. Often they use very different languages that have evolved in the course of distinct histories.

The content of the above paragraph represents, I suggest, the soft underbelly of liberalism.[5] Despite a plethora of reasons to be sceptical about truth claims (some listed above)—liberals believe that truth is to be had, and it seems in many ways, they believe that it may be discovered independently of any consideration of the divine. To them, derivation of truth is not dependent on the intervention of any divine being. People on their own thinking in empirical ways which nature has provided can, according to liberals' understanding, think their way to truth.[6]

I suggest that to many people in the world, such a notion of human self-determination, of truth based on nature, would sound like an enormous myth. Perhaps more importantly, it can be taken as a great deception. It can be a grandiose way of trying to excuse extreme narrow mindedness: "listen to me!" I will come back to that shortly. Fauconnier and Turner tell us that the mere perception of a cup of coffee requires profound engagement of the human imagination.[7] Human beings have a free will and an imagination—where exactly can we draw a line between these things and

---

3. Goffman, *Frame Analysis*.

4. All the above can be in place even if the communicating communities are of one culture. Of course two communities are never exactly of "one culture"; people's personal life experiences and accumulated life orientation always affect how they interpret new cultural information.

5. I am aware that liberalism is a slippery, much used, and very broad term that is "employed in a dizzying variety of ways in political thought and social science" Bell, "What Is Liberalism?", 682. I use it to refer to modern trends in political thinking. I assume with Siedentop (*Inventing the Individual*, 332) "that in its basic assumptions, liberal thought is the offspring of Christianity. It emerged as the moral intuitions generated by Christianity were turned against an authoritarian model of the church."

6. My mention of "divine" has here already brought us a problem. The West has been running with a dualistic worldview that we are here critiquing. In that dualistic view, there is a category of divine or "not real," and a category of "real/nature." People are of necessity put into the latter "real" category. Yet people are capable of functioning in ways that can seem very contrary to "nature." The categorization of people as non-divine on the side of nature begs the question of just who or what is "divine."

7. Fauconnier and Turner, *Way We Think*, 8.

what might constitute the "divine"? Could it be that the divine resides in the imagination? Kaufman speaks into this question, noting that there is a role for the imagination in serious philosophical thought as well as in prayer:[8]

> The mind's ability to create images and characterizations, and imaginatively to weld them together into a unified focus for attention, contemplation, devotion, or address, is at work in the humblest believer's prayers as well as in the most sophisticated philosopher's speculations. In this respect all speech to and about God, and all 'experience of God,' is made possible by and is a function of the constructive powers of the imagination.

What divine speaks anyway, except through a person? Even should a voice emerge from the sky, for it to be understood by someone it still has to communicate in a way that can make sense to a human being. Whether a vision or dream comes from someone's imagination or from a god: are the two all that different? Are they clearly distinguishable? Perhaps they are to certain stripes of modern western Protestantism? Not everyone finds them so easy to distinguish. When the imagination plays a part in the formation of truth and meaning, as according to Fauconnier and Turner it does,[9] then truth and meaning are no longer entirely based on "nature." My reader should recognize that distinguishing between divine intervention and human imagination parallels distinguishing between the religious and the secular that I have already discussed in detail in chapter 1 and beyond. More on this when I look at Tanya Luhrmann's work below.

The presupposition that the distinction between divine intervention and human imagination is clear is only really spread through European languages. It may be taken as a true presupposition amongst educated people in much of today's world, when they are functioning in "educated English." That does not mean, however, that it is true to perceived reality outside of western Christianity. I suggest from experience of observing "divine activity" in parts of Africa that the human imagination is very much involved. Luo people, according to their traditions, perceive of God as being in somebody. Hence Mboya tells us "*Nyasaye lak mana e ringre dhano*" (god moves in the body of a person).[10] The thought that God is somehow "out there" is not universal amongst those who profess faith in God. God might also be "in here," i.e., in the person, functioning as an essential part of the person.

8. Kaufman, *Theological Imagination*, 22.
9. Fauconnier and Turner, *Way We Think*, 6.
10. Mboya, *Richo ema*, 17.

That makes a bit of a mess of the dualist notion that a person belongs on the natural side of the presumed natural versus supernatural (or secular versus religious) divide. Of course it also causes us to ask again: who is god? This, as I have already suggested above, is the critical question, not the question of "whether God exists," the answer to which in this sense is obvious to the non-Westerner. Questions regarding the nature of God are of such critical importance to a non-Westerner that we cannot afford to be deflected from them by queries arising from the western worldview regarding his existence. It is only by narrowing the understanding of "who God is" that so-called atheists have been able to postulate God's non-existence. (This latter point is well made by Reitan.[11]) I have already indicated above that it is co-identifying God and "supernatural" that seems to have caused many to reject "faith in God." Those who so reject such faith presumably consider Christians to "believe in the supernatural." Supernatural is a category arising from western dualism which most African people do not grasp. Hence on the above basis it would be supposed that most African Christians do not believe in God! (I reiterate this point here due to its centrality to the thesis I am developing.)

We have suggested above that the imagination in a person includes ways in which the divine reveals himself. Whether we call it imagination, or whether we call it "the divine," I suggest that something of this nature is indeed a genuine part of what it is to be human. It is a part that can and does profoundly influence the rest of life, in very important decisive ways. As such, as with other parts of life, I suggest that it needs attention. As we have specialists in functioning of the digestive system, in use of language, and every other field of human behavior, so we ought also to have specialists in the field of human imagination/the divine. This is something that liberals seem to disallow. A few examples will illustrate this. When Appleby began researching the question of fundamentalism, fellow scholars apparently expressed no patience with what they considered to be "religions" and "religious issues." The sentiments they expressed can, according to Appleby, be summarized as follows: "If we are going to give this much money to the study of *religion*, then the project should help to wipe it off the face of the earth."[12] Pinker and Goldstein similarly appear to have no time for those who would deign to engage in the important task of orienting

---

11. Reitan, "Moving the Goalposts," 81.
12. Appleby, "Rethinking Fundamentalism," 227.

people's "imaginations," preferring "pure reason."[13, 14] Green in his look at AIDS articulates the horror expressed by his colleague at Harvard University in the USA at the thought that he may take the Pope seriously.[15] Such behavior from people who are supposedly serious scholars is puzzling. Do they expect the human imagination to disappear, for us to remain as "men without chests" as Lewis put it, as a result of their obstinacy?[16] They seem to be denying a role for imagination in human understanding. If only! As a person passionate about human flourishing[17] I find the imaginative component of people's thinking to be one of the most difficult areas to deal with. At least in the African context I am in, the work of the imagination all too often results in disunity being the order of the day. Teachings found in the Christian Bible have a phenomenal part to play in bringing people together in a way that can bring diverse imaginations into check. That is, the gospel provides a kind of boundary for the imagination. In my home area, a high proportion (I do not have statistics) of people meet together with others at least twice a week with the primary purpose of worshipping God and thanking him for his goodness. To write off a massive chunk of human existence as somehow superfluous seems like academic and theoretical suicide—yet it appears that swathes of contemporary liberals have done just that. The outcome of their scholarship ought as a result to be suspect.

Perhaps most ironically of all, those who want to deny a role for human imagination (i.e., the divine) are themselves historically rooted in some very specific contexts shaped by the "imaginations" of their predecessors, that enabled their own existence and development. Liberalism itself arose from Christianity.[18, 19] "Like many others, he [Siedentop] insists that something about the content of Christianity must have been decisive in making modern Western beliefs possible," Moyn tells us in his review of Siedentop.[20] "If we look at the West against a global background the striking thing about our situation is that we are in a competition of beliefs whether

13. Pinker and Goldstein, "Long Reach of Reason."
14. For more on this, see below.
15. Green, *Broken Promises*, ix.
16. Lewis, *Abolition of Man*, 34.
17. For which purpose I carry out Christian ministry.
18. Smith, *Short History*, 153.
19. See also Siedentop, *Inventing the Individual*, 332 cited above.
20. Moyn, "Did Christianity," and Siedentop, *Inventing the Individual*.

we like it or not."²¹ "Liberalism rests on the moral assumptions provided by Christianity. It preserves Christian ontology without the metaphysics of salvation."²² Many of its tenets are clearly borrowed directly from the church. Liberals owe an enormous debt to Christianity. Christianity denies neither the divine, nor the imagination, so how then can liberals?

It is saddening to think how many liberals have failed, in their dealings with Africa, to realize so much about the imaginative/divine leading of Africa contexts. Even Christians from the West carry a lot of suppositions in common with their more liberal western counterparts, but at least they do also engage in the spiritual sphere, and in that sense have a holism about them. That holism can act as a bridge between the West and Africa. Such a bridge is not there for liberals. I do not know how many of them realize the kind of complexities involved in intercultural communication that I have articulated here and elsewhere.²³ Liberals seem to forget that so many of the values that they hold dearly are acquired as a result of faith in Christ.

Liberalism provides little if any defence against the aggressive encroachment of radical Islam.²⁴ Hence with reference to the Arab Spring, Tony Blair tells us that while the "liberal minded . . . [may be] . . . numerous . . . [they are] . . . badly organised."²⁵ It is Christianized areas of Africa that have been able to resist the encroachment of Islam. In many parts of Africa one has to be either Christian or Muslim. This identity determines the nature of necessary rites one goes through (such as weddings or funerals), clothes one wears (especially for women), food one eats (does one share in the fast of Ramadan, for example), who one is encouraged to marry, with whom one is likely to do business, and so on.²⁶ Someone who fails to take on an identity as a Christian that can resist Islam typically has little choice but to be absorbed into Islam. (Liberals who deny their Christian roots have no foundation from which to defend their resistance to Islam. They have little or nothing to tie them together to arrive at a concerted position.) This feature of life tends to be concealed to Westerners who, as explained

---

21. Siedentop, *Inventing the Individual*, 1.

22. Ibid., 388.

23. Notably in my book entitled *Communication in Mission and Development*.

24. "Islam is not a peaceful religion" says Murray, frankly, in his report. (http://www.spectator.co.uk/2015/01/religion-of-peace-is-not-a-harmless-platitude/).

25. http://tonyblairfaithfoundation.org/religion-geopolitics/commentaries/opinion/depth-challenge.

26. For more insights on this, see Meagher, "Trading on Faith," 400–406.

LIBERAL INTERPRETATIONS

above, overtly consider themselves to be making on the basis of "nature," decisions that are actually arising from their Christian faith.

This issue takes us back to the confusion as a result of which non-western ways of life have been considered to be "religions." Considering them to be "religions" has caused Westerners to have certain understandings of what non-Westerners do, and why. One of these foundational but misguided understandings is that non-Westerners do what they do because of what they deeply believe. To try and simplify what is all-told a very complex reality, in many parts of the world "belief" by a few (perhaps very few or even none at all[27]) can determine the nature of rites which others are then pretty much obliged to follow just so as to function normally in a community.[28] That is to say, all the men who attend an event at a Mosque may not "believe in Allah or Muhammad as his prophet" at all, yet pragmatically speaking to prosper in their community they are required to attend Islamic prayers. Asad makes this clear when he tells us that Muslims are little concerned what one actually "believes" in one's heart, as long as one behaves appropriately in public and says the right things.[29] I notice a similar thing in my life in an African community with respect to "fear of the dead." When the life of a community of which one is a part revolves around activities rooted in fear of dead people, then one has little choice (unless one wants to be a lonely social misfit) but to participate in activities that seem to suggest that one fears the dead, whether or not one believes that the dead can "do anything." (Fortunately or unfortunately, rites based on fear of the dead tend to be subsumed into rather than to resist either Christian or Islamic structures.)

Once a people have submitted to Allah,[30] it has typically become very difficult for them to pick up values that many liberals hold dearly. This fact

27. It is presumably possible for no-one to actually "believe" in the system that guides their community, but at the same time for no one to be able to speak out. To take the example of Muslim belief, because anyone who speaks out against Muhammad is quickly condemned yet Muhammad's life sets the pace for Muslim practice, one cannot know just how many people are towing the line despite having no heart-felt conviction that the way they are following represents absolute truth.

28. This is because there is no place in "nature" from which such necessary rites can emerge.

29. Asad, "Freedom of Speech," 289.

30. The meaning of "Islam" is "submission," as noted by Claire Stevens when her son became Islamic. She comments: "The word Islam means submission. It allows you to love nothing else; to be a good Muslim, you must surrender yourself completely." (http://www.spectator.co.uk/2014/10/my-boy-the-radical-muslim/.)

53

takes us back yet again to chapter 1 of this book: Islam is not a religion, yet for liberalism to flourish it needs to be complemented by a religion.[31] The same can be said for modernism or secularism. "Islam seems to sit uneasily with secularism."[32] Hence in non-Western (i.e., non-originally-Western Christian—as explained by Huntington[33]) contexts we get different versions of modernism, like the Afro-modernity described by Comaroff and Comaroff.[34] There are almost certainly many additional reasons for liberalism to struggle to flourish under Islam, all of which I cannot go into now.

I do want to consider the prominence and role of liberalism in yet more detail by focusing on a few authors. George Yancey looks at "academic bias" in America.[35] Yancey finds political conservatives and so-called "religious" people to be grossly under-represented in academia. This applies especially to some social/arts areas, but also to a lesser extent to the sciences.[36] He asks how this imbalance arises. Self-selection may account for a lot of the difference. Certain Christians seem to be voluntarily opting out of academia, presumably because they prefer other career outlets. Perhaps academia somehow repulses them? Perhaps they self-select out of academia for a complex number of other reasons in addition. "My theory does suggest a bias that eliminates the consideration of ideas that do not fit into a culturally progressive, secularized viewpoint" Yancey tells us.[37] Christians may "face exclusion from certain academic programs" according to Yancey.[38]

By confining itself to liberals the academic world seems to be responding to an invented notion of the "real world." That is to say that in the actual "real world," people are much more influenced by conservative

---

31. Chapter 1 looked at some misleading uses of the term "religion." The content of the term in English and other western languages is rooted in Christian belief. To call "Islam a religion" is to say that it is Christianity but by a different name, something which may actually not be the case at all.

32. Siedentop, *Inventing the Individual*, 350.

33. Huntington, *Clash of Civilizations*, 20.

34. Comaroff and Comaroff, "Notes on Afro-Modernity," 331.

35. Yancey, "Recalibrating." No mention seems to be made of the fact that his study is American-based. Part of his bias is the implicit assumption that somehow the USA legitimately represents the world. Others have noted such a bias in other discipline areas. "It seems problematic to generalize from industrialized populations to humans more broadly, in the absence of supportive empirical evidence." Henrich et al., "Weirdest People," 69.

36. Yancey, "Recalibrating," 270.

37. Ibid., 277.

38. Ibid., 272.

ideology than academia likes to accept. One must surely question the legitimacy of academia's claims to be independent of things that are at the same time a part of their own supporting fabric. For example, could liberalism be considered truly comprehensive were liberal academics who get sick to be cared for by conservative nurses who are motivated by their faith in God?[39] In other words: in "real life" it may be that liberals cannot actually do without some of the things they claim to deeply hold to be superfluous. Someone living in a high-rise apartment who denies the existence of soil does not thereby make farmers' fields disappear. Within the confines of the apartment, their faith may be upheld, but it will fail if they travel more widely. Meanwhile, even while in the apartment, they are eating food grown in soil. Could academics be turning out liberal theories as a result of intense (albeit unintentional) bias? Screening conservatives out early in the career process can be "an important mechanism by which culturally progressive academics are able to maintain a comfortable social atmosphere, since they do not have to deal with the arguments [or the lifestyle witness] provided by cultural conservatives or the traditionally religious."[40, 41] The benign social atmosphere of academic senior common rooms may be more about exclusion than truth or representativeness.

Yancey does not deny that conservatives might be being actively excluded from academia. Perhaps a confessing Christian is less likely to be recruited into an academic position. Yancey also suggests that conservatives may be screened out before they ever get established. Efforts at ascertaining whether there is bias in academia by assessing the progress made by conservatives is pointless if the bias is actually working itself out in the form of exclusion, even if by self-selection. Either way though we need to ask: can academia be considered to be either impartial or representative of a population, if such biases are so foundational to its basic constitution? Yancey's paper seems to confirm that much of academia is not rooted in objective knowledge but in exclusionary practice. Are academics achieving agreement by excluding those who do not agree? Which way exactly are we heading if this is the basis of the expertise that guides contemporary countries and peoples? Is this the basis for academia's refusal to take God seriously?

Perhaps Losurdo will give us the most biting critique of liberalism. Liberalism is supposedly grounded in the liberty of the individual, Losurdo

---

39. See Siedentop above.
40. Yancey, "Recalibrating," 277.
41. The term "culturally progressive" is apparently used as a synonym for "liberal."

tells us,[42] but how does that flesh out in practice? Losurdo's historical study denies the popular *hagiography* of liberals. To Losurdo, any effort by liberals, typically Anglo-Saxons from America and from England,[43] to achieve freedom for certain individuals, came on the back of slavery for the rest. For Losurdo—liberalism and slavery were "twin births."[44]

Calhoun, according to Losurdo, believed that Blacks could survive in conditions of being slaves.[45] As far as Losurdo is concerned, John Locke himself had no compassion for "primitive people."[46] His liberalism and liberalism in general were only to benefit free persons, not people in general.[47] That is, heads of households were to benefit. Members of households, including women and slaves, received no freedom-rewards. Slavery thrived under liberalism, and would have continued to thrive if the church and the crown had not sought to undermine it.[48] As early as 1537, according to Losurdo, it was the Pope who was acting against slavery by prohibiting the giving of sacraments to those enslaving Indians.[49] Not everyone accepted the legitimacy of such interference.[50] The general view in the eighteenth and nineteenth centuries was that non-European people were barbarians and deserved no better than slavery.[51] Hence Theodore Roosevelt was of the opinion that supreme races had the right to "a war of [non-European people's] extermination."[52]

Losurdo gives a very clear message regarding liberalism. That message is: for all the benefits that liberalism may or may not have to offer, alone it is cruel. Liberalism needs a counter-balance to blunt its ragged edges. This applies regardless of liberalism's own self-laudatory claims of pre-eminence. In North America, and presumably a number of other places, Christianity has provided that counter-balance. Hence for all their agitations to the contrary, liberals in western countries cannot do without

---

42. Losurdo, *Liberalism*, 2.
43. Ibid., 248.
44. Ibid., 302.
45. Ibid., 2. See also Calhoun, *Union and Liberty*.
46. Losurdo, *Liberalism*, 24–25.
47. Ibid., 25.
48. Ibid., 28–34.
49. Ibid., 305.
50. Ibid.
51. Ibid., 223–240.
52. Ibid., 330–331.

Liberal Interpretations

religion, i.e., Christian populations, to keep them in check.[53] This seems to bring us right back yet again to the dualistic model we looked at in chapter 1. Western Christianity has been ready to give room for something in its midst that is not Christianity. That has been liberalism (using our current terminology). Liberalism can provide a complement to Christianity. However, the West's presupposition that other "religions" can have the same role and give room to liberal ideologies as does Christianity is where they have been misguided. In reality, Christianity, particularly western Protestant Christianity, is the model on which the category of "religion" that implies complementarity to liberalism or secularism, is based. Therefore, other people's ways of life, for example Islam, Hinduism and so on, are NOT religions, and do not in this sense behave as "religions." Note also that Christianity can spread "organically" from one human community to another; Christianity includes means to spread itself, i.e., many Christians are motivated to share their faith with others. When it so spreads it can set a foundation that can allow liberalism considerable wiggle room. Liberalism only spreads effectively where a particular western brand of Christianity has, so to speak, preceded it to till the ground. Whatever variety of liberalisms ought to be there in the future, I suggest that they must grow out of and function alongside Christianities. Liberalism needs a close association with something indigenous. It cannot be the basis for its own intercultural spread. That indigenous "thing" is an indigenous church. The West, in the interests of Africa and the majority world's benefiting from any positives inherent in liberalism, should prioritize spreading the means for the development of indigenous Christian churches.

One might want to suggest to liberals that they ought to fulfil a helpful complementary role to Christian belief. Their origins being in the church, that would seem not such a surprising thing to propose. On the contrary though, contemporary liberals like to claim exclusivity. Many liberals do not consider themselves to be a complement to religion.[54] They are more likely to want to do away with Christianity, rather like Richard Dawkins himself. (See examples given above, and examined in more detail below). I suspect that the unwillingness of liberals to play "second fiddle" is a major weakness of liberalism. Certainly Christians struggle at times with the au-

---

53. In the USA "science is unable to remove religion from its role as ethical arbitrator and guide" according to Smith's analysis of America's "culture wars." Smith, *Short History*, 40.

54. I use the term religion here to refer to Christianity.

thorities they are put under. Yet the Christian faith incorporates a critical advocacy for humility and accepting the authority of others that liberals may be lacking.[55] Do liberals need Christian belief to keep their more extreme innate human nature in check? Throughout history one role of the church, often through relating to governing bodies, seems to have been to keep selfish practices in check.[56]

I will look again in more detail at the two examples, mentioned in passing above, of apparently mainstream narrow mindedness on the side of liberals. One is revealed to us by Green in his look at how "the AIDS establishment has betrayed the developing world."[57] (This quote is part of the title to his book.) Green reports ways in which his liberal colleagues mocked and derided any notion that perhaps they ought to listen to the Pope, and that perhaps the Pope knew (or knows) better than they did.[58] Green, it seems exceptionally for a liberal, found himself making the same case as the Pope: "In 1988 I first advocated the inexpensive common sense strategies I have fought for ever since. Millions of men and women would still be alive if we had followed them [instead] we—global AIDS programs—have ignored the prevention methods that help while wasting billions on strategies that don't."[59]

Another example also comes from Harvard University, this time from Steven Pinker and Rebecca Goldstein. In 2014 they produced an animated TED talk entitled "The long reach of reason." Watching this on YouTube, I was quite incredulous at the disparaging remarks made with reference to what Pinker and Goldstein call "religion." Goldstein talks disparagingly about "the appeal to religion to justify the otherwise unjustifiable, such as the ban on contraception" as the kind of thing our grandchildren will in the course of history be horrified by. Pinker adds to this "what about religious faith in general?" (implying that it all needs to be got rid of).[60] To this Goldstein responds that "I am not holding my breath." Differences in opinion are pretty normal amongst scholars, and others, but one might expect

55. For example Biblical passages like Phil 2:3–4 and 12–13 advocate for humility.

56. This is not to say that selfishness and being bigoted are not problems for Christians. That they are problems for Christians does not negate the above. Christians strive, by the very nature of what it is to be a Christian, with the help of God's spirit, to overcome such things.

57. Green, *Broken Promises*.

58. Ibid., ix.

59. Ibid., xi.

60. Pinker and Goldstein, "Long Reach of Reason."

better than such belittlement and mockery. The Pope and or Christians in general, are portrayed by the above as pea-minded bigoted idiots, apparently intent on seeking to oppress on the basis of a groundless faith! Why such vicious attacks? Why so little understanding?

There are many ways one could endeavor to explain the above animosity. I will take just two such. One, that liberals are subconsciously aware that they have particular theological roots, and are building on particular theological foundations. While they are also adept at concealing those foundations, they will not go away. I draw here particularly on Lewis who tells us with respect to a "secularized" person that once having rejected the Tao[61] (i.e., in Chinese "the way," which is to say, "the reality beyond all predicates") "however far they go back or down, they can find no ground to stand on."[62] Values are not conclusions, but premises, says Lewis.[63] For Lewis "the rebellion of new ideologies against the Tao is a rebellion of the branches against the tree."[64] A secularized person realizing that they have "no ground to stand on" implies of course that the possibility of the existence of "ground" is known, as a branch will sense there must be something called "tree." We have seen above how Asad has begun to uncover roots of secularism by sharing how religion, and therefore secularism, are not universal default categories, but creations of particular forms of Christianity.[65] They hide those foundations, because they like to deceive themselves into believing that the foundation they are building on is somehow natural, objective, and therefore theoretically universal. Second, as also mentioned above, liberals have, by excluding conservatives from the academic senior common room, lost the voices that could and otherwise would question. This seems to be much about human nature, and not much about good scholarship.

"Godless" liberal prescriptions for Africa are, I suggest, typically too misguided. They provide little by way of a bridge to inherent traditional African understanding. But then, so may be some more conservative prescriptions. Many western Christians seem to presuppose that western dualism is already there in Africa rather than trying to introduce it or to advocate it. What does the appropriate middle road look like?

---

61. Lewis, *Abolition of Man*, 18.
62. Ibid., 77.
63. Ibid., 53.
64. Ibid., 56.
65. Asad, "Construction of Religion," 122.

5

Inventing Godlessness Amongst Christians

IN THIS CHAPTER I want, in order to give an example of the logical conundrums created by western dualistic ontologies, to focus on the work of Tanya Luhrmann. Luhrmann is an anthropologist, currently working at Stanford University, USA. Luhrmann writes about Christians and their beliefs, while presupposing that God does not "exist."[1] She holds onto this foundational presupposition with a gritted determination despite attending churches and church fellowships for years on end. Having this kind of stand is accepted procedure for a professional anthropologist. I would like to explore what can happen when someone who maintains secular presuppositions takes a close look at Christianity. I find her research to be absolutely fascinating, if also mind-boggling. Of added interest to us in this book is her comparative work, whereby she compares North America and England with India, Thailand, and more recently and of particular concern to us, Ghana in Africa.

Luhrmann presupposes a particular understanding of God amongst her target research group. As an academic she can disqualify this understanding using science, so as to lay a framework for [objective] research. Thus she necessarily identifies herself as being a member of an "open

---

1. I take God's not existing as being that he is not "real." Luhrmann does not do this glibly. I do not suggest that she is somehow naive about her assumption of God's not being real. (See Luhrmann, "Talking Back," 389–92, to see some of her discussions concerning this topic.)

society."² This seems to parallel anthropological practice with respect to sin that I look at in another recent article.³ Sin can be understood in different ways. Traditionally for Christians (and presumably others) sin has had much to do with the breaking of God-instituted taboos. Sometimes it is difficult or even impossible to understand the reason for such taboos using human reasoning. Recent centuries have focused much on the capability of human reason, to such an extent that even Christians have come under pressure to show how their faith is "reasonable," and to deny aspects of it that appear not to be subject to reason. Hence, to an extent, Christians have jettisoned taboo-based understandings of "sin" that go beyond their reasoned understanding. Their Christianity has become a following of what makes rational sense. Western Christians, probably particularly Protestants, have valued such reasonable prohibition of sin, and perceive it as coming from the Bible and from Christian tradition. In due course, anthropologists acquired access to "primitive people" who had apparently only recently had contact with Judeo-Christian faith. The anthropologists wanted to find out: do these people's traditions include prohibitions against sin? This was not a neutral investigation. "Anthropology addresses the same subject matter that religion has traditionally addressed," according to Hallowell.⁴ At the same time the anthropological fraternity has long been somewhat anti-Christian. They have "developed [their] . . . ideas in part in opposition to, and as replacement of, Christian views of mankind."⁵ Research on "primitive peoples" was a means of trying to win points "against Christians." When Margaret Mead writes about the Samoans, she is explicit in telling us that her book will "give the reader some conception of a *different and contrasting civilisation*, another way of life, which other members of the human race have found satisfactory and gracious" (my emphasis).⁶ When Mead, found that "primitive people" (in her case, Samoans) did not seem to prohibit sin in the way that did Christians, this seemed to be a great victory for anthropology, secularism, and liberalism in general over the apparently unnecessary prohibitions made by Christians, especially of

---

2. Horton, *Patterns of Thought*, 222. Horton makes a very overt reference to dualism: "In traditional societies there is no developed awareness of alternatives in the established body of theoretical tenets; whereas in *scientifically oriented societies*, such awareness is highly developed" (my emphasis).

3. Harries, "Sin v. Taboo."

4. Hallowell, "History of Anthropology," 22.

5. Priest, "Cultural Anthropology," 86.

6. Mead, *Coming of Age*, 12.

sexual promiscuity.⁷ I argue in my article that the reason the anthropologists did not recognize sexual prohibitions they were looking for amongst the people they investigated was because they were looking for "sins" based on reason, whereas traditionally even in the West prohibitions were based on taboo.⁸ One ongoing impact of pronouncements made in that era is that some people still today take Christians as "kill-joys."

The above anthropologists did not realize the need for what we could call *sub-rationality*, i.e., in other words, "taboo-based" prohibitions for the effective functioning of human society.⁹ They were rather assuming the universality of a category "religion,"¹⁰ and that the category was "total illusion."¹¹ (Evans-Pritchard points out that this has long been the habit of many anthropologists.¹²) They were wrong to think that rational means alone are adequate for the setting of a foundation for human thinking. Yes, rationality comes into play, but it cannot be foundational. Luhrmann recognizes this in citing Horton who pointed out "that neither the African accounts . . . nor the Western scientific accounts . . . are common sense models of the world."¹³, ¹⁴ The necessity for something that is beyond the rational to set the foundations even for "rational" living is an important point to bear in mind.¹⁵ Rationality is as a result of necessity built on foundations that are other than rational!

Luhrmann does not question the dualistic distinction believed by the West to be foundational to a correct understanding of the world. In a sense her dogged determination to hold onto such belief is sad. In another sense it is fortuitous. This is, as I have already mentioned above, because it is in so far as Luhrmann represents many Western people who are just as dogged in their determination to hold fast to the bone of dualism, that her writing can

---

7. Priest, "Cultural Anthropology," 94.

8. Harries, "Sin v. Taboo," 159.

9. Compare here "imaginative operations of meaning construction" going on below the surface, according to Fauconnier and Turner in *Way We Think*, 15.

10. Renowned anthropologist Geertz presupposed the existence and reality of a category "religion," defined by him here in "Religion As a Cultural," 90.

11. This illustrates anthropologists' clear positioning of themselves on the "real" side of the dualistic distinction we have already much focused on in this book.

12. Evans-Pritchard, "Religion and the Anthropologist," 162.

13. Luhrmann, "Hyperreal God," 371.

14. The words I quote here are Luhrmann's, which she writes in response to Horton, "African Traditional Thought."

15. Harries, "Sin v. Taboo," 168.

be taken as genuinely anthropological. Had she left her course and become a theologian, the anthropological fraternity might have removed her from their exclusive guild, and liberals might have written her off: "In present academic practice, the question of whether a given author was theologically motivated or free of all such parochial interests continues to be asked, explicitly or implicitly, whenever any writing on religion is evaluated."[16] In other words, we could almost say that she has taken the position of Pharaoh with the hardened heart of Old Testament fame (Exod 9:12). Luhrmann's investigations could, I believe, help us out of certain ruts arising from modern thinking into broader understandings of Jesus' revelations and plans for mankind.[17]

Drawing theological insights from anthropological research could be seen by some as playing with fire, or at least as working backwards.[18] At the same time, contemporary theologians increasingly recognize that context has a big part to play in their task. I would like to challenge people regarding the place of Christian faith in human flourishing. Globalization has already brought many challenges to majority-world peoples, perhaps especially Christian believers and churches. This chapter presents such. I believe that as kindling to a fire so is truth to the vigor of Christian belief. I hope that readers of all persuasions will come away from reading this chapter newly invigorated, even if slightly less modern and western in their presuppositions than when they started.

I propose that Luhrmann's ideas are meaningful to the extent that they flow out of the dualist thesis that is a major focus of this book. I use Luhrmann for this exploration because dualism is a constant theme throughout her writing. "How can people find meaning in something

---

16. Masuzawa, *Invention of World*, 69.

17. In a similar way to that recorded in Matt 4:1–11 whereby the devil's questions helped Jesus to set the course for his ministry. (A parallel account is also recorded in Luke 4:1–13.) In Matthew's Gospel we find Jesus being tempted to 1. Turn stones into bread. 2. Throw himself down from the highest point of the temple. 3. To fall down and worship the devil. Jesus sets out the course of his ministry through refusing each of these temptations.

18. It must be said though, that the Christian faith has not been averse to the use of eclectic sources to supplement its own knowledge, going back to biblical times. For example, Moses seemed to be very happy to accept advice from his father-in-law (Exod 18:24), a priest of Midian and not of the God of the Bible Yahweh (Exod 3:1). This eclectic nature of Christianity can prove frustrating to atheists, as pointed out by Reitan who was accused of "redefining religion so that it no longer matches the target that the new atheists attack." See Reitan, "Moving the Goalposts?", 81.

unreal" is one of the implicit foundational questions to her research. This very question presupposes that the categories of real and unreal are themselves "real" (to use Horton's terms, already cited above, that such an "awareness of alternatives" between scientific [real] and non-scientific [non-real] is legitimate[19]). She does not, to my knowledge, question that presupposition. As a contemporary academic she must, to fulfil convention, put God into the "unreal" category. If he does not fit into the "real" category, then according to western thinking he must be "unreal." If he is unreal, then to Westerners that means that he does not exist, which means that "believing in him" is folly. A parallel dualism in Luhrmann's thinking is that of "in the mind as against out of the mind."[20]

Luhrmann implicitly raises the question of whether Christianity is a western faith or a global faith. In those parts of sub-Saharan Africa with which I am familiar, people do not hold to the dualisms that Luhrmann presupposes disqualify Christian belief (because they render God "not real"). She realizes the same herself and I guess is trying to come to terms with its implications. Yet it is not without reason that undermining of the kinds of dualisms mentioned in the above paragraphs has implications for all Westerners, whether or not they claim to be Christians. Many western Christians rest their faith on God being in the real as against the unreal category, on his being supernatural as against "natural," and on his being external to the human mind yet able to communicate with it "from the outside."[21] If categories of "real" and "unreal" are abolished, then on what basis does a Christian believe? Atheists similarly seem to rest their faith on the reverse being the case, and the outcome of abolishing "real" versus "unreal" is the same for them as well, that is, on what basis does one "not believe"? It is to me ironic that so many Westerners consider these contingent modern western-produced categories to be necessary foundation stones to their faith in God, or their faith in not God.[22]

Some key questions raised above are missiological in nature. An important question implicit to much western mission effort to Africa,

19. Horton, *Patterns of Thought*, 222.
20. Luhrmann, "Talking Back," 396.
21. Luhrmann et al., "Absorption Hypothesis," 71.
22. These websites illustrate the concern amongst English-speaking Westerners with the question of whether God is "real": http://www.charismanews.com/opinion/43192-seven-things-that-prove-god-is-real, and http://isgodreal.org/. I do not mock this concern. The concern does demonstrate the necessity for cultural foundations of a particular people to underlie their faith in God and in Christ.

although this question is rarely overtly asked, is: Are Africans required to become dualists in order to become "proper" Christians?[23] Much evangelistic, missionary and development work engaged from the West implicitly presupposes a "yes" answer. Western Christians in particular rarely see their implicitly held dualism as a contingent cultural feature. In my experience, they simply take it as being "correct" and universal. This implies that not-dualistic African churches are not truly Christian. They are in need of evangelism, conversion, or at least correction from the West. Consider the fact that even after decades or hundreds of years, Westerners continue to see African Christians as needing tutoring and educational and other inputs from the West.[24] Much theoretical work may still be warranted looking at this issue. In my view though the answer is clear: God is greater than dualisms! Refusing to acknowledge this would be to verify, apparently at least, Luhrmann's suspicion that Christianity can be explained from the category of real without having to evoke belief in a real God. That is to say, Luhrmann, as other anthropologists, goes about explaining "religious" behavior in "this-worldly" terms. They do this, by assuming that the human mind is entirely not-of-God,[25] and that the supernatural, the only arena in which they allow God could convincingly reveal himself in order to be "god" and not science or nature, is not real. This is where the western church, which has tended to itself follow the above logic, might have much to learn.[26] Its greatest lesson may be the need for humility. Then might come a re-writing of some theological text books.

Just to add briefly here what I will also come back to below; the danger of assuming that languages translate interculturally. Dualism being strongly implicit to the English language (see chapter 4 above) makes it very difficult

---

23. Luhrmann implicitly assumes that legitimate belief in god includes the notion that God (god) is somehow "outside of" the mind, and is supernatural as against natural.

24. While many African churches have been in Kenya for one hundred years or more, theological education institutions typically teach in English using textbooks written in the West.

25. Which leaves imagination "floating" (drawing in part on Lewis, cited above in chapter 4).

26. This is an issue for the western church, which the eastern church does not share (Ware, *Orthodox Way*, 46). The contemporary sharp distinction between real and unreal is very much western (Huntington, *Clash of Civilizations*, 70). Hence, according to Derrida, scholarship has boomed in the West: "There has never been a scholar who, as such, does not believe in the sharp distinction between the real and the unreal, the actual and the inactual, the living and the non-living, being and non-being." Derrida, *Specters of Marx*, 12.

to sensibly articulate non-dualistic reasoning using English. Other European languages are presumably the same. This calls for much wisdom. Discarding dualism may be to totally undermine modern economics, which would have much to say about "development." Upholding its apparent (apparent to Luhrmann and other convinced secularists) implications may be to set apart the non-West as a permanent underclass to the West. I now want to examine some of Luhrmann's work in more detail. I have not read all her work, but I believe enough of it to give us a good discussion.

CHURCH IS GOOD

Luhrmann informs us of research that has shown clear benefits to churchgoing for Americans. "Weekly church attendance keeps people healthy . . . [it] adds two or three years to one's life" according to a study in the USA.[27] Luhrmann reports that "religious observance [i.e., church attendance] boosts the immune system and decreases blood pressure" so "the way God is understood also affects health outcomes."[28, 29] She goes on to say that there is evidence "for the claims that an interactive relationship with a loving God cultivated through the imagination in prayer, may contribute to good health."[30] There appears to be a disconnect here: how can the (real) activities of imagination and prayer contribute to a (real) "interactive relationship with a loving God" (who is not "real")? "Following Mary Watkins we might call these "imaginal" relationships:[31] they require the imagination, but are not necessarily imaginary" Luhrmann suggests.[32] Nonetheless, Luhrmann goes on to add that mental health workers should see "the relationship [i.e., Christian faith] of their clients" as being something positive.[33]

---

27. Luhrmann, "Making God Real," 707.

28. Ibid., 707–08.

29. Luhrmann in one paragraph cites four different research reports, by Hall (in 2006), Hummer et al. (1999), Koenig and Cohen (2002), and Woods et al. (1999).

30. Luhrmann, "Making God Real," 708. Assuming here that imagination and prayer fall on the "real" side of the real versus unreal dichotomy, but point to a loving God who is not real.

31. Watkins, *Invisible Guests*.

32. Luhrmann, "Making God Real," 708.

33. Ibid.

Inventing Godlessness Amongst Christians

I have done a little maths that may be of interest! "Weekly attendance at religious services accounts for an additional 2 to 3 life-years."[34] Let us assume that "religious attendance" for 20 years qualifies for the above improvement. Simplifying a little, if the above research is correct, then someone spending two hours in church on Sunday for twenty years will achieve a life extension of 2.5 years, that is an extra 105 hours of life for every hour spent in church. That's quite a good payback. Perhaps that should be on a church's billboard: "Sit an hour in church for a four-day life extension!" No one would want church services to end! Church might go on for five hours, or even longer. Well, in Africa, church services can go on for five hours or more. Perhaps we are already learning about African Christianity? It is about life and its propagation and prolonging—qualitative and quantitative. Perhaps then the African view works the other way round to the envisaging of the West. That is—instead of looking for God and then seeing how he can "help" someone, they might look for what helps, then call it God. That means of identifying God does not seem to raise the same questions the West struggles with regarding his being "real" or "unreal."

Luhrmann identifies benefits to believing in god as if God is a means to therapy.[35] Western Christians may object to such. It sounds very much like the prosperity gospel, about which many western theologians are very wary.[36] So they should be wary: but perhaps another important question is: what is to be done about the prosperity gospel and the African inclination to value God for what he can give them, if the African worldview does not distinguish real from "unreal" in the first place? It can seem plainly obvious in Africa that God should indeed provide material prosperity, probably because this is by definition in Africa what God does.[37] Does God have to fit into Western categories, i.e., be "real" (i.e., not unreal) to be believed in? If not, then Luhrmann would have to concede that: in churches people do indeed worship God. That would make Luhrmann and many other academics into theologians, something that contradicts the [objective] dualistic framework they must presuppose in order to maintain their credentials. Luhrmann's research seems to arrive at theology through the back door. It exposes the gross vulnerability of the very foundations of anthropology and other "secular" disciplines to shifts in theological understanding.

34. http://www.ncbi.nlm.nih.gov/pubmed/16513898 (accessed November 9, 2015).
35. Luhrmann, "Making God Real," 721.
36. For example, see Cotterell, *Prosperity Theology*.
37. I explore some of these ideas in more detail in Harries, "Name of God."

THE GODLESS DELUSION

To some Westerners, the above discussion may be mind-blowing. Yes, the West is making moves towards being "holistic." A well-known missiological journal in the UK, *transformation,* is sub-titled "an international journal of *holistic* mission studies" (my emphasis).[38] The Micah network strongly promotes holistic mission.[39] Do these and other related organizations, who seem to be taking a step in the direction of interrogating the dualistic framework presupposed by the West, realize the full implications being explored here of what they seem to be advocating?[40]

SCIENTIFIC APPROACH TO THEOLOGY

One aspect of Luhrmann's scientific approach to understanding people's interaction with God is her drawing on psychology. She does this very openly and unapologetically in her 2010 article by having a psychologist as co-author.[41] This has her yet again strongly engaging the dualistic paradigm. She compares Christian prayer to the "making-real" process being engaged by a shaman (the shaman talks in such a way as to help the patient to realize the "reality" of the spirit causing their misfortune).[42] She adds; "if you put aside the theological purpose and supernatural efficiency of prayer, prayer . . . helps to make what is imagined more real."[43] This "blurs the boundaries between what is external and what is within between what is real in the world and what is imagined through the Scriptures" she adds.[44] A child's attachment to their teddy bear demonstrates the "psychic domain from

---

38. http://trn.sagepub.com/.

39. http://www.micahnetwork.org/integral-mission.

40. Various things may be intended by the use of the term "holistic," which may not always be totally in line with our suggestions on how to overcome issues raised by incipient levels of dualism. For more on this see Harries, "Material Provision."

41. Luhrmann et al., "Absorption Hypothesis," 68. Luhrmann is herself "trained in psychology" (http://luhrmann.net/).

42. Luhrmann, "Making God Real," 710. "The shaman helps the woman to experience the spirits as real by drawing her attention to them and telling her that they are real; incorporating them into the narrative without any break from the previous realistic description; giving them vividness; and creating interaction." Luhrmann's use of the term "real" in this context I think is a little unfortunate. Perhaps she uses the term real in a sense of being brought to the fore in one's mind, rather than as one of two categories in a dualism.

43. Ibid.

44. Ibid., 713.

which creativity, art and religion were born" suggests Luhrmann.[45] She concedes that boundaries can "blur," which seems to be an accommodation of something non-dualistic, but finds that an aberration rather than a norm. She locates the source of Christian faith in the mind yet seems to never seriously consider that perhaps *God himself is in the mind*! In case some might think she has ventured too far from objective reality, Luhrmann is careful to clarify that "technically such experiences are called hallucinations"[46] and "Spiritual experience is akin to psychic illness."[47]

In her 2012 article looking at the absorption hypothesis, Luhrmann again draws heavily on psychology in order to understand how the "real" and "unreal" interact with each other. She looks at theory developed in development psychology, which considers the development of the minds of little children in a way that takes account of the context in which the development occurs.[48] She then looks at the evolutionary psychology school that "seeks to identify the features of mind that can be plausibly attributed to supernatural beings."[49] Then she looks at perspectivism, the theory that draws on the assumption that "humans and nonhumans are understood to have . . . similar minds."[50] Dualist western Christians may be rather depressed and perhaps totally foxed through reading all the above. Is this because their belief is based on a dualistic assumption that God is external to the human mind, and impacts on the mind from the outside?[51] Luhrmann herself finds the universalism of such belief seriously challenged when she turns to her comparison with other nations and cultures.

Phenomenological method was supposed to underlay research which aimed to discover comparative "experiences of the supernatural" between the USA and Thailand.[52] On reading this account, it seems to me to be an attempt at comparing American belief in God with Thai belief in what Luhrmann chooses to call the supernatural. The way supernatural is translated into the Thai language is described as "something that's not human,

---

45. Ibid., 715.
46. Luhrmann et al., "Absorption Hypothesis," 72.
47. Ibid., 74.
48. Luhrmann, "Toward an Anthropological," 9.
49. Luhrmann, "Hyperreal God," 382.
50. Ibid.
51. Cassaniti and Luhrmann, "Encountering the Supernatural," 46 and 50.
52. Ibid., 38.

without a body, a spirit, an invisible being."[53] As a teacher of theology with extensive experience teaching in Dholuo, my mind boggles trying to conceive of how such might be understood by Dholuo speakers in Kenya.[54] How then might this kind of translation be understood in Thailand? We are told that "76 [out of 158 asked] people reported personal encounters with the supernatural (i.e., with 'something that's not human, without a body, a spirit, an invisible being')."[55] Then we are told that one response "seemed to counter the idea of the supernatural as distinct entities [that are] no longer really alive."[56] The issue the Thais seemed to have was not with a "supernatural," even when carefully explained as above. Instead they were concerned about energy and about mindfulness.[57] To them, anything that might resemble the supernatural appeared not to be outside themselves at all. To them "the mental energy of other minds intermingling with one's own—created the *supernatural*" (my emphasis),[58] and was their concern. The western dualistic category of supernatural does not fit the understanding of the Thai people.

Luhrmann realizes that there was something different going on in Thailand by comparison with America. "God [in America speaks] as an external and distinct person-like being" Cassanati and Luhrmann noted.[59] He appears not to do so in Thailand.[60] Luhrmann proposes that this points to "differences in the understanding of mind."[61] Thus the notion that a person is an autonomous being enclosed in a bodily shell is "a conceptualisation particular to a Western context" (according to Mauss[62]).[63] We are back to dualism being a western peculiarity. Westerners are clearly wrong to think that their understanding, that anything "supernatural" has to origi-

---

53. Ibid.
54. I will come back to language and translation issues in more detail below.
55. Cassaniti and Luhrmann, "Encountering the Supernatural," 39.
56. Ibid., 39.
57. Ibid., 40.
58. Ibid.
59. Cassaniti and Luhrmann, "Encountering the Supernatural," 46.
60. As I noted above, with reference to Thailand, Luhrmann tends to use the term "supernatural" rather than the term God. It would seem that the reason Americans perceive God as an "external and distinct person" is because their underlying dualistic cultural presuppositions dictate that understanding to them.
61. Cassaniti and Luhrmann, "Encountering the Supernatural," 46.
62. Mauss, *Category*.
63. Cassaniti and Luhrmann, "Encountering the Supernatural," 50.

nate outside of the human mind, is universal. We need to ask ourselves: is this western distinction correct? Does the Christian faith stand or fall on the basis of some notional western understanding of God being exterior to the mind and a part of a supposedly real world? Has the West thus defined itself out of faith in Christ, resulting in some people being able to "choose not to believe"?[64] Perhaps, and if so, we now know how.

If "correct" Christianity is dependent on one's having a dualistic conception of the natural and the supernatural, then I suggest that we do not have Christian churches in Africa. The notion of "supernatural" depends on there being an understanding of "natural" which something may endeavor to become "super" of. Yet the notion of nature or natural held by the West, as something that is neither God nor miracle, is not an African category. Therefore neither can supernatural be an African category. The same can be said of the mind. The notion that God has to emerge from outside of the human mind is in a sense, I suggest, an untenable one. A human only comes to perceive anything at all using their mind. I perceive everything using my mind. I must perceive God using my mind. That is: God will come to me through my mind. In that sense he will be "in" my mind. There is no other way.

Luhrmann writes about another intercultural exploration in her 2015 article on "hearing voices." This time the subjects of study are those people who would according to American understandings be considered to be schizophrenic. "Other cultures" have people whose behavior resembles those identified with schizophrenia in the USA. So according to Luhrmann: schizophrenia "occurs across cultures in identifiable ways."[65] Luhrmann decided to explore the reported nature of the voices heard by various "schizophrenic" people in different cultures. Americans disliked the voices they heard, found the voices to be aggressive, and considered them to be not-real. Ghanaians found the voices they heard to be good and telling them to do good things. In India the voices heard were thought to be kin speaking to the schizophrenic person—generally making the hearer happy to be in communication with the departed.[66] Luhrmann draws on a theory of *social kindling* in which she assumes that certain social factors are responsible for what is happening. "The theory of social kindling lays down a research agenda" she says "to identify the ways in which cognitive

64. Smith, *Short History*, 47.
65. Luhrmann et al., "Hearing Voices," 647.
66. Ibid., 657.

bias (about minds and mental events in interactions with persons and spirits) might affect the way persons in different social settings report spiritual experience and respond to specific objective probes (e.g. what people hear in ambiguous noise). That work is underway."[67] It seems that Luhrmann is launching out on a theological investigation in all but name. Due to the dualistic framework required by western academia, however, centuries of wisdom concerning issues like the discerning of spirits will most likely not be considered.

Cross-cultural investigations about "voices in one's head" may still be in their early stages. Yet anthropologists have here staked a claim to expertise. Based on my understanding that anthropologists often consider themselves as little concerned about moral issues,[68] I expect the research to privilege the "friendly" voices of Ghana and India. Luhrmann, for the time being at least, seems ready to ignore the evils of "friendly" voices that identify witches and point to malevolent spirits that can be extremely troublesome in my home area of Western Kenya, and beyond. Usually people dealing with these issues are theologians who examine the nature of gods, and what that nature ought to be. I fear that Luhrmann's claim to being an authority may reduce the "authority" of alternative voices who have good cause to say things that are different to that which Luhrmann has discovered at this particular stage in her research. In other words: Luhrmann's ignoring theological advice risks encouraging people who take her seriously to play with fire. Amongst the people at risk of getting burnt by the fire (i.e., ignoring of seasoned advice regarding how to respond to people with voices in their heads) are many in Africa. Is this an attempt at usurping, i.e., attempting to trump, the authority for example of the Christian Scriptures and centuries of experience acquired over many generations of human history? Is this advisable? In other words: the marginalization of indigenous theologies potentially opens a door to "real world" repercussions which are hidden through a process of theorizing from a dualistic perspective. In the interest of promoting human flourishing, I suggest it is immoral to ignore the risk here entailed.

To restate concerns of the above paragraph in a different way, while it may be nice to think that voices in one's head are friendly, western academics may be told that this is the case due to fear that repercussions from the same may be untoward if people say otherwise. That is, Ghanaian people

---

67. Ibid., 659.
68. Winter, *Frontiers in Mission*, 44.

may fear that talking against the voices could result in the perpetrators of those voices taking revenge.[69] There appears to be no basis in a morally-neutral dualistic perspective for considering potential evil impacts of such voices, or the evil that someone may attempt to perpetrate through a pretense that they are hearing voices. Causation in holistic societies is always connected to people.[70] That includes causation of misfortune.[71] "Voices" who falsely accuse, or even correctly accuse in some cases, different people of causing someone else's misfortune may be extremely destructive to peace and harmony in a community. "As anthropologists we should not lightly endorse claims that diviners possess powers of extrasensory perception. An insufficiently critical stand leads us to ignore the problematic role of diviners in fomenting anxiety, and in authenticating accusations that have led to brutal killings, in South Africa and also in Tanzania."[72] This is one of the foundations for the evil associated with witchdoctors, who in trying to help people with their problems can make unfounded or unhelpful accusations that generate and perpetuate deep interpersonal antagonism between members of a community. In the words of Niehaus: "anthropological studies can ill afford to adopt an uncritical, purely interpretive, stance towards witchcraft and divination."[73]

IMAGINATION AND LANGUAGE

Questions regarding language, translation and understanding are extremely pertinent to this intercultural research. Without great care, the effects of translation between Ghanaian, Indian and Thai languages could, I suggest, effectively nullify some of Luhrmann's investigations. At the very least I suggest she needs to use fellow Americans to translate for her from those foreign contexts, and not only to rely on the indigenous knowledge of English of local people.[74] For her work in Thailand Luhrmann is assisted by a tourist who became a doctoral student.[75] It is not clear how familiar the

---

69. Spirits overhearing what someone is saying may not appreciate being considered to be evil. (See also Harries, "Intercultural Dialogue," 181.)

70. Richmond and Gestrin, *Into Africa*, 35.

71. Manala, "Witchcraft and Its Impact," 1498.

72. Niehaus, *Witchcraft and a Life*, 212.

73. Ibid.

74. See the final chapter of this book section 2, page 136, for more on this.

75. Cassaniti and Luhrmann, "Encountering the Supernatural," 40.

doctoral student is with the Thai language and how the Thai people use it. In India Luhrmann uses indigenous people to conduct and then report to her on their research.[76] In Ghana, an indigenous research assistant helps her to do interviews in non-English languages, i.e., in Twi.[77] I suspect that might be why she has been told that the voices people have been hearing are "good." When it comes to reporting African findings to Europeans (in which category I include North Americans), pleasing people may be more critical than western notions of truth.[78] Hence I suggest that if a researcher wants accurate information, at the very least he *must* use fellow Westerners with long, deep and profound local knowledge to be his translators. I suggest also that researchers base their research on participant observation.[79]

I concede that I do have a vested interest in this issue—but I should say also a legitimate one. I have myself lived since 1988 at grassroots level in an African community. I use the local African language fluently on a daily basis. I continue to live now in the same community that I first came to in 1993. Westerners are variously very active in my home community, including researchers who always prefer to work with English-speaking locals. That is the politically-correct procedure. This has a number of drawbacks:

1. The nationals engaged will often have a limited comprehension of what the researcher is looking for.

2. Nationals will have social, family and other obligations that take priority over research objectives.

3. Research assistants will be carrying ways of understanding so foreign as to be basically incomprehensible to a typical western researcher. Working with such people could unfortunately result in the creation of castles in the sky.[80]

As a member of a community one is expected to say and do things that are in the interests of the community. Foreigners proposing projects or research almost invariably are in one way or another powerful players. Such is certainly the reputation of white people in Africa: it is very rare to find them involved in things that do not imply power—money, salaries,

76. Luhrmann et al., "Hearing Voices," 646.

77. Ibid.

78. There are many reasons for this to be the case, not least economic dependency of Africa on the West.

79. Harries, "Pragmatic Theory," 88–107.

80. Harries, "Building Castles."

reputation, influence, prestige, increased knowledge of international languages—all these and more are likely to be at stake for the Africans helping with western research. In such a context, relationships between powerful outsiders and locals can be a very tricky balancing act. Outsiders must be *very* wise. Much wiser than, unfortunately, in my experience, they often are. They particularly need to realize how community members must at least be perceived to speak and act in the interests of the wider community, and ways in which this has a higher priority than some western notions of "truth." The greater the power, or perceived or anticipated power, of the foreigner, the less important it may be to tell the foreigner "truth" and the more likely people are to endeavor to tell them what they want to hear and what is most likely to bring them some kind of reward.

I want to go on to imagination. This discussion would be much more complex, profound, and true to context if I was to be able to decipher how non-western-English-speaking people understood what we tend to consider under the category of imagination. English as a language has dualistic foundations. These have arisen over years of scientific input. The English term imagination is no exception. Imagination is regularly considered to be on the "real" side of the dualism. Few native English speakers would argue that someone having an imagination proves anything about the existence or reality of the "divine." Yet, products of imagination may well be considered to be on the "unreal" side. The term "prophecy," the term that would seem to describe "imagination that is real," on the other hand, is not a term that would be considered credible in mainstream circles. Other cultures and languages do not make these same distinctions.

Luhrmann's position rests on the maintenance of contemporary native English categories of thought and, as a result, language. For Luhrmann's thesis to stand, imagination must *not* originate in the divine. Luhrmann's research, as a result, becomes a self-fulfilling prophecy—if one starts out with the assumption of the absence of the divine, then facts will become victim to that assumption, and the divine will not be found. (This of course is why as a Christian one has to begin with faith. Hence Heb 11:1 and the following accounts of "faith.") Unfortunately, as I have mentioned above, beginning with such a (actually groundless or arbitrary) presupposition can be risky, if only because it seems to disqualify ways in which people have guided their affairs for centuries. One also needs to ask oneself: why should research be taken seriously if the foundation on which it is building is arbitrary? I ask: is imagination necessarily distinct from "divine intervention"?

Pretending that people simply and easily fall on the *natural* side of the natural versus supernatural or real versus unreal divides is, I suggest, a travesty.[81] Human beings can have a roving and wild imagination. Am I in total control of my imagination? No. On the contrary, my imagination often takes me to places that I had never anticipated. Who (or what) then exactly controls my imagination? It seems to be a being in me that is not me. Dreams, presumably closely connected to the imagination, illustrate this. I have occasionally found myself in a half-awake state, in which I was dreaming, and at the same time capable of consciously following what is happening in my dream. Many things are happening, often very quickly, in that dream. I, my conscious self, am not directing what is going on. Who or what is? What is that in "normal" people, if it is not the "divine"? This is of course a matter of definition. Other explanations for this "agency" exist. To separate people totally from the category of divine, as if people are entirely "natural" beings, seems a mighty stretch. I propose therefore that Luhrmann's use of English in her research, especially when it looks at intercultural contexts, valorizes a western paradigm which is not relevant cross-culturally. English is too partial.

I seem to have stepped up this debate by disqualifying a whole language! Luhrmann actually does a very similar thing. She concedes, for example, that questions on "the divine" in Thailand do not evoke notions of atheism. Even if the divine (i.e., the supernatural, to use Luhrmann's term) is invisible,[82] that does not result in Thai people's questioning its existence.[83]

The above short discussion opens up a massive vista! Were Sapir and Whorf correct in suggesting that language is determinative?[84] That

---

81. This brings to mind the passage in John's Gospel, John 10:34–36, which apparently cites Ps 82:6, suggesting that people can be considered to be "gods" (θεοί) in a sense that is not blasphemous (verse 36). (NIV used). Note also that the Hebrew word *Elohim* (the term found in Ps 82:6) is translated "judges" in Exod 21:6 and 22:8, 9, and 28. Gen 1:27 tells us that people are made "in the image" of God. From Gen 2:7 we discover that the very life-essence of people comes from God.

82. Cassaniti and Luhrmann, "Encountering the Supernatural," 38.

83. There seems to be no suggestion in the account on Thailand that the "supernatural" either does not exist or does exist—because what the Thai people know is something different from the North American definitions of "supernatural." (Ibid., 39.) This fact does threaten to undermine Cassaniti and Luhrmann's research somewhat. In the broad sense of the "supernatural," i.e., as the Thai themselves describe and understand whatever it is, they do not seem to doubt it.

84. "The Sapir-Whorf hypothesis is the theory that an individual's thoughts and

is a complex question to answer fully in a small space. In short—it is the language/culture combination I suggest that is "determinative," not simply a language by itself. That is to say—Thai people (for example) could use English to express their own culture, but English people reading or hearing that Thai use of the English language would not by those means alone grasp Thai culture, i.e., what that Thai person is talking about. Similarly, hearing or even using English will not alone transform Thai culture into English culture. The old gods will remain. This means that English descriptions of Thailand will be using non-Thai categories, so in that sense will always be "wrong," as will Thai descriptions of England. What does that make of Luhrmann's careful ongoing division between the real and unreal, on which she bases her arguments? It makes it into an intracultural issue. It seems to mean that what Luhrmann is discovering is something peculiar to Western people that arises from the peculiarity of the categories that they assume in their use of their languages. This means, as already intimated, that any absence of the "divine" in the West originates in the West. It arises from western people's being trapped into their own "culture." It is by no means universal. If it is not universal, one has to question if it can be "real," and if it is not "real" then the West's case collapses. That takes us back to the old perennial question of "what is god(s) *like*?", the traditional and perhaps more useful and relevant question for us to address instead of the question of "is god real?". This is a question that anthropologists as well as other academics avoid.

Interestingly, Luhrmann realizes that in Africa "religion is everywhere—and atheists are few."[85] Charismatic Christians in Accra "imagine a world swarming with evil forces that attack your body, your family and your means of earning a living" Luhrmann tells us.[86] Some North Americans *imagine* God as a person external to themselves. Other North Americans *imagine* God as shut out behind an imagined real/unreal distinction. If all we have in our world are "imaginings," well, that is exactly the context(s) that the Bible addresses. The Bible does not presuppose science. Science came, in many ways, after the Bible. The Bible speaks to imaginings. It speaks, that is, to people who live in a world in which "imaginings"

---

actions are determined by the language or languages that individual speaks" (https://linguistlist.org/ask-ling/sapir.cfm).

85. Luhrmann, "When Demons Are Real."

86. Ibid. Clearly western interpretations of Africa, such as this one, tend to transfer western presuppositions to African contexts, resulting in an impression of evil forces coming to people's bodies and minds from the "outside."

(the divine) are as real or unreal as non-imaginings, if there are any such thing. That is to say: the Bible is its own foundation, or in other words it is founded in God, which means that it provides a basis onto which further thinking can be constructed. It is in so many ways *the* basis on which everything else the West has, has been constructed. (A clear case for this is made by Mangalwadi.[87]) The post-modern West again finds itself in a world in which imaginings cannot easily be distinguished from non-imaginings. That is the context that recognizes the arbitrariness in absolute terms of the assumption that there are real things and not real things. I suggest that, once one has rejected the Bible that points towards such a distinction, no foundation remains for accepting it. This is a point that I take Derrida as making.[88] Mangalwadi demonstrates how European values and European technology including science (i.e., European notions of what is "real") have all emerged from centuries of study of and of following of the Bible: "the bible inspired Christians to devote their lives to recovering God's forgotten mandate for humans to take dominion over nature."[89] If it is the Bible that has allowed the West to draw a distinction between real and unreal in the first place, then it hardly seems right to use the same distinction to discredit the very Bible.

My above sentence ought to remind us of another key theme in this book—that of religion. Western scholars have and frequently still *do* take religion as some kind of universal. We have discovered above that the category is variously defined, but comes down to being "something like Western Protestant Christianity."[90] That is, a Christianity that accepts the legitimate existence of the secular. Let us say, western Protestant Christianity's God is such that he allows or even encourages the secular. This is why sharing about Christianity is the necessary prerequisite for the majority world (i.e., the non-West) to achieve *sustainable* economic and social development. It is a question of theology. The only true "religion" therefore is western Christianity. Use of the term to describe other things quickly becomes misleading, as it can make those "other things" *appear to be* western Protestant Christianity.

Anthropological research in general, as well as other "secular" disciplines, rest on the assumed existence of a category called "the secular."

---

87. Mangalwadi, *Book That Made*.
88. See chapter 6.
89. Mangalwadi, *Book That Made*, 221.
90. Asad, "Construction of Religion," 122.

That category emerged from western Christianity. Therefore, Luhrmann's experiments at assuming that God might not be in the equation, originate from God. This is a self-contradiction. It is this self-contradicting nature of her work that I point to.

CLOSE TO HOME

My choice of Luhrmann's materials was not a random pick off the shelf. I have been impressed from the start with her detailed efforts at understanding how Christians function in practice. I became even more interested when I heard of her recent involvement in Ghana. I guess that is because of parallels between her research and my own research. As a theologian, I find myself engaging, often on a daily basis, with many of the issues she writes about. I have also carried out a lot of research in anthropology, although looking at things in a different way to Luhrmann. At one point I went for an interview to do a PhD in anthropology.[91] I turned down the offer, preferring to prioritize theology. The decider for me was that I wanted to be located on the field. The anthropology PhD would have forced me to spend many more years at a UK university, whereas a degree in theology was much more enabling of actually living in Africa and engaging closely with African people.[92] So, I am a theologian who makes much use of anthropology while working in some ways similarly to Luhrmann. My objective is to spread and share the word of God. Ironically it seems from reading Luhrmann that her own objective is not actually all that different.[93]

Luhrmann's comments about the Sumbanese, actually an Indonesian people and not an African people, are especially interesting to me. Luhrmann reports on a researcher who studied certain missionaries who encouraged the Sumbanese to use their own language in their Christian expression.[94] "This made the Sumbanese Christians exceptionally uncomfortable" Luhrmann recounts based on Keane's work, "and they did all

---

91. In Manchester, UK. I believe it was in 1993.

92. I did an MA in Aspects of Biblical Interpretation at London Bible School (now London School of Theology) in 1994/5. I later wrote my PhD in theology (drawing heavily on other disciplines including anthropology) between 2003 and 2007.

93. As I have mentioned above, Luhrmann is looking at a "theory of mind" (Luhrmann, "Hyperreal God": this phrase is part of the title to her article), which seems to me to be very much like "a theology."

94. The researcher was Keane. For example see Keane, *Christian Moderns*, 89.

they could to avoid these local reminders on the grounds that they might bring the pagan spirits back to mind and possibly into active life."[95] I have observed such at times amongst the Luo of Kenya, although many others have overcome this difficulty and are happy to use their mother tongue in Christian practice.

This does further illustrate what I have already alluded to above—the association that can be there between language of use and the nature and activity of the gods. English portrays God in a certain way. Some missionaries have been frustrated when their efforts at inculcating "theological English" into African students have been frustrated. I suggest that this can be because English is a secular language. While "secularism" is a known term in Kenya, this does not mean that African students have grasped what it is to be secular in the western sense. There are many interpretations of the term "secular."[96] Amongst educated African Nairobi residents, I discovered that "secular" can mean "back to the ancestors."[97]

As Keane wrote of the Sumbanese so I could say of the Luo, that even though missionaries got some things "wrong," one still does not find Luo people "grappling with disbelief in the supernatural."[98] Luhrmann talks of a "playful epistemology."[99] American evangelical Christianity has "a playful, self-consciously paradoxical framing of belief-claims in which God's reality is both clearly affirmed and qualified" Luhrmann tells us.[100] If I understand her rightly, then I have observed the same in the West. That is, that western Christians live in a kind of tension in which the logic of their culture that they essentially accept can seem to undermine their Christian faith. That is to say: some (or most?) western Christians are very familiar with arguments that seem to do away with a need for God, even at heart level. Yet they are at the same time convinced Christians. We could say that they combine belief and disbelief.[101] They can joke about belief. It is as if

---

95. Luhrmann, "Hyperreal God," 381.

96. Calhoun et al., "Introduction," 5–6.

97. In a personal conversation with a scholar in Nairobi, I was told that secularism was on the rise in Nairobi, Kenya. Further careful listening on my part revealed that the term "secularism" was being used to refer to the practice of people's own traditions, especially as arising from respect for and fear of the dead, as against the practice of Christianity.

98. Luhrmann, "Hyperreal God," 381, drawing on Keane, *Christian Missions*.

99. Luhrmann, "Hyperreal God," 381.

100. Ibid., 371.

101. Ibid., 383.

Inventing Godlessness Amongst Christians

their lives do not depend on it. This is not true for Sumbanese Christians according to Keane (as articulated by Luhrmann), or for African believers. For them their lives do depend on God.[102] That kind of belief often attracts Westerners and is appealing to them,[103] but they struggle to put themselves there. We have been looking at some of the reasons for this struggle.

In a paradoxical way, visibility or even audibility of the divine seem to play only a marginal role in promoting faith. Seeing is not needed for believing, let us say. That is not to say that seeing might not encourage faith. On the other hand—because faith is other than in seeing, seeing might actually confuse. We could helpfully think here back to the Thai above. Luhrmann failed to find the kind of notion of supernatural that she was looking for amongst the Thai. One monk suggested that talking of the supernatural was a waste of time![104] A Westerner might on that basis conclude a person who says such to be secular, or "of no religion." Yet they would be wrong to think that such a person is now like a western secularist. We are told that there are no secular people in Asia.[105] Thailand gives us a clue of how this might work. Luhrmann reports for the Thais that "the mental energy of their minds intermingling with one's own—created the supernatural."[106]

What Luhrmann considers a theory of the mind, is really incredibly close to what we could alternatively call a theology. Theology after all is

---

102. For example, the Sumbanese hold to a belief, according to Keane, that "prayers will bring about material results" (*Christian Moderns*, 15), a belief the seriousness of which proved to be problematic to Calvinist missionaries.

103. A good example of a Westerner's admiration for the "simple faith" of converts coming from non-western traditions is given by Tippett, in *Integrating Gospel*, 223–38.

104. "When she first asked him [Nan Jon—an ex-monk] about the experience of the supernatural, he was reticent to talk about it, saying, 'Buddhist monks don't talk about this stuff. There's better things to do with your time.'" Cassaniti and Luhrmann, "Encountering the Supernatural," 39.

105. Madsen, "Secularism, Religious Change," 266.

106. Cassaniti and Luhrmann, "Encountering the Supernatural," 40. Pages 40 to about 46 of Cassaniti's article are to me a translation debacle. The above sentence; "the mental energy of their minds intermingling with one's own—created the supernatural," should in my opinion, for purposes of cultural honesty, be translated something like the following: "The mental energy that is not mental energy of their minds that are not minds (as known in the West) intermingled (being one term that just begins to describe the actual extant relationship between minds and energy) with one's own, given that to say 'with one's own' may be as misleading as it is helpful, created something which with a major stretch of the imagination might just be labelled as 'supernatural' using the dualistic language English, even though 'supernatural' is really a far cry from what Thais would actually have had in mind."

"words" (*logos*) about "God" (*theo*). It is about how one ought to best understand the gods/God/mental energy, or whatever label we should use for that which is extant in Thailand. Christians believe that God has left us with some directions, the following of which take us closer to a right and good way of living and human flourishing. In other words, to use Luhrmann's terminology, Christians operate by a particular "theory of mind."[107] By all accounts, that theory of mind is phenomenal; 32% of the globe's population consider themselves to be Christian.[108] Thus they hold an allegiance to that "theory of the mind." The allegiance may be variously strong or weak. It may at times even seem to be forgotten in people's lives, but it reappears at critical junctures, and suddenly becomes the deciding factor in what to do and how to do it with respect to critical human behavior.[109] An example that I recently heard comes to mind: Angela Merkel, president of perhaps the most powerful of the nations that form part of the European Union, clearly based her motivation on opening the door to refugees on her Christian faith.[110] The fact that the European Union is apparently secular did not deter her from doing this. Major world-changing decisions are being made contemporarily on the back of faith in Jesus Christ, that is on the back of a certain "theory of mind."

It is Christian countries, especially those of western Europe, which have brought "development" to the globe. They have been the ones to introduce science and develop it and enable its wider spread. Science functions in European languages. Science builds on the divisions between the real and unreal that arose out of western Christian theology. I don't have space here to comment on whether perhaps science has been desirable or otherwise. It is incredible to me to observe such an enormous revelation of truth arising on the back of Christian belief. I do not mean absolute truth—I am not sure that science falls into that category. But certainly a functional truth. There is little doubt that science has revolutionized a lot of functionality of late especially in communication, enabling means of communication previously unheard of.

---

107. "Theory of mind" is part of the title of Lurhmann's article, "Hyperreal God." See also the same article, page 372.

108. http://www.pewforum.org/2012/12/18/global-religious-landscape-exec/.

109. "Very frequently the 'world images' that have been created by 'ideas' have, like switchmen, determined the tracks along which action has been pushed by the dynamic of interest" said Max Weber, in *From Max Weber*, 280.

110. http://www.liveleak.com/view?i=fb6_1441776541.

Inventing Godlessness Amongst Christians

A Christian "theory of mind" is certainly having a massive impact on Africa. Outside of the parts of the continent in which Islam has become entrenched, it seems that myriads of African churches are spontaneously springing up all over the shop. Unlike almost everything else "new" on the African continent, many of these are independent of outside funding or control.[111] Yes, foreign funding is coming into African churches, but it would certainly be my observation that, perhaps increasingly, the multiplication of churches is continuing independently of outside subsidy. A case can be made to say that outside funding that invariably results in efforts at imposing unfamiliar ways of thinking is handicapping church growth. African people are very aware of the importance of having the right "theory of the mind," and are rushing to it in their droves. Churches "pop-up" everywhere. They are not churches of atheism, liberalism, or of godlessness, or of westernization, or of anthropology, but churches that seek to practice the Christian faith.

---

111. Dependency on outside aid is an issue also in churches. Yet, I consider churches to be in a league of their own, as almost the only western originated institution in Africa that has acquired "local momentum"; there is Christian activity that is clearly not westernization. This arises because the Bible itself that underlies the Christian faith is pre-western, or supra-western. In other words, because the church draws its strength from God, who is universal and whom African people also appreciate, African churches can become truly indigenous in a way that few if any other institutions can achieve. This situation seems to extend also way beyond Africa: "The indigenous churches in northern Argentina" Paul tells us "are among the few spaces left in the life of the local indigenous communities where members and leaders are free to make their own decisions." Paul and Paul, "Serving As Guest," 90.

6

Fortune For Atheists

AFRICAN PEOPLE WANT TO prosper; so one could say do most people. Probably all people! The search for prosperity or good fortune is widespread and pervasive wherever one goes.

Dualistic Westerners have focused their search for prosperity on the "real" side of their dual view of the world. Attempts to locate fortune in the physical material world that is understood as operating on scientific principles have been extended from people's material contexts to people themselves; even study of people has come to be seen as if it is a scientific exercise. Disciplines like psychology tend to be very quantitative and data based. Study of people as social creatures has endeavored to follow the example of science; hence we have social *sciences*. Few disciplines in western universities seem to have escaped this trend. God as a source of prosperity has become marginalized as a result of, inside and outside of the humanities, the above focus on what is considered to be the "real." This has been part of the process of secularization.

We can note in passing that African people are not in the same scientific "trap" as is the West above. There is an important sense in which African people's perception of the source of human flourishing *is* that which is often translated into English as god.[1] I suggest that there is an iterative relationship between the content of flourishing, and the nature of God; both of these constantly impact on one another. African approaches we are considering are therefore built on a broader foundation than is the

---

1. I use "fortune" as a partial synonym for human flourishing, so as to capture some of its traditional and contemporary African links to the content of "luck" and "chance" as found in secular western worldviews.

secular or liberal.² Their approaches are tried and tested over millennia as being: that which works. Unfortunately, widespread subservience of God to pragmatics has in the past limited "that which works" in certain ways.³ Revelations about the actuality of God expressed in the Bible and communicated by the church are enabling African people to break out of a spiral of necessary-pragmatism. Such is enabling forward-looking perspectives that reflect directions taken over centuries by the western world. These include freeing people from the necessity to take revenge and from the fear of the mystical impact of the envy of others, and by perceiving the possibility of self-less love. Changes in comprehension of the nature of God shift avenues of articulation of what works. This latter is an extraordinarily enabling role of the church.

Having stated the classic view of secular society as being rooted in a worldview very limited to the material side of a contemporary dualism, we can very quickly qualify the same view. Perhaps only a small percentage of people even in Europe actually hold the above position. Even in supposedly secular Europe, research shows that 77% or more of the population consider themselves to be Christian.⁴ North America is a particular mystery to many Europeans: the USA is undoubtedly a western nation, but in which the church is comparatively strong and influential.⁵ These kinds of statistics ought to make one wonder what is really going on. Are claims of secularism pretentious? Is secularism widely known as being Christian? Is Christianity and its "very real" influence and spread for some reason being concealed?

2. African approaches are broader than the secular or liberal on the basis that secular and liberal efforts to achieve flourishing deny certain aspects of human existence, such as human imagination, as already discussed above.

3. I can try and illustrate this point. By subservience of God to pragmatics, I mean that in Africa God has been sought for and understood for pragmatic purposes. Options of understanding of God that do not bring results in a relatively short-term are as a result rejected. This is one reason why African people can be said to be so enthralled by the Bible. Use of the Bible, i.e., faith in the God of the Bible, opens up options of understanding of God that bring long-term reward despite apparent short-term drawbacks. Monogamy may be an example of such. In the short term, it hardly seems to be in a man's interests to limit his options by permitting himself only one wife. In the long-term, a strong tradition of monogamy can enable depths of relationship and flourishing that result in positive changes to society as a whole. Hence having God's word or the Bible as an authority can be the source of many positives.

4. Halman, *European Values*, 81 and 86.

5. http://www.huffingtonpost.com/2014/02/15/americans-more-religious_n_4780594.html.

Statistics that record religious observance usually look at church attendance.[6] In recent times, many experiences once available only by physically going to a church gathering, are accessible to people in their homes; sermons, friendships (e.g., Facebook), discussions on key human issues, homilies expounding on the Bible, giving to charitable causes, and even congregational singing can now be had through internet, radio, TV, and other electronic media without actually going to church. Reduced church attendance clearly does not necessarily mean reduced adherence to Christianity. It could even mean the contrary; contemporary media can bring the best of Christian expression to people's living rooms, when in the past people had to make do with their mediocre home-church pastor. A lot seems to be at stake. We have already above explored ways in which people who enter academia tend to be liberals. Similar things could probably be said about the media. What might have changed in the West is not so much adherence to Christianity, but its expression, and the way it is reported.

Christian perspectives are intertwined with the historical development of western civilization. Berman found the origins of western legal systems to be firmly rooted in Christianity and in the church.[7] So then, he asks, given this origin, are western legal systems truly "neutral"? How can they be neutral, if they have arisen as a result of centuries of influence of a particular understanding of God arising from the Bible? Epistemologically we need to concede that legal systems cannot be neutral—because there is no "neutral" or "natural" base from which they could originate. There is no choice but for legal systems to have arisen from insights given by and perspectives imported from "god(s)."[8] The apt question pertains to the nature of that god (or gods).

Similar discussions have been engaged regarding the origins of human rights. The declaration of human rights claims an impartial neutrality. Ingram clearly shows how it originated in particular historical contexts.[9] He demonstrates that human rights have a very "distinct history." They are not the products of "nature or reason as their authors like to proclaim, but of politics."[10] The context of politics in Europe that has shaped the derivation of human rights has been profoundly influenced by Christianity over

6. http://www.encyclopedia.com/doc/1G2-3045001056.html.
7. Berman, *Law and Revolution*.
8. See especially Siedentop, *Inventing the Individual*.
9. Ingram, "Revolutionary Origins."
10. Ibid., 9.

many centuries. Hence the universal declaration of human rights is also profoundly of Christian origin. "Human Rights [is] firmly anchored in the DNA of the Christian Faith" confirms Schirrmacher.[11]

I suggest that the contexts of the above two paragraphs are totally unacceptable in the modern world. A great deal has been invested in suggesting that what I am claiming above is not true. To say a "great deal" may be an understatement. Secularists have been advocating political policy globally on the basis that it is founded in common sense and impartial wisdom. Hence democracy is promoted globally by international bodies that claim to have no particular adherence to Christianity. So Bhargava tells us that Christianity is these days spreading incognito: according to Bhargava, western secularism "presupposes a Christian civilisation that is easily forgotten because over time it has silently slid into the background. Christianity allows this self-limitation, and much of the world innocently mistakes this rather cunning self-denial for its disappearance."[12]

I would like to suggest that Islam's overt opposition to Christianity is one reason why Christianity frequently spreads incognito. Despite being of Abrahamic origins, Muhammad's example has left people following a very different way of life to that promoted by Jesus in the Bible. Muhammad's example results in a way of life that the Christian West struggles greatly to value. Many Westerners find many of the values of belief founded by Muhammad to be "consistently negative."[13] Blommaert and Verschueren's research revealed that, with respect to Islamic immigrants into Belgium: "the tolerant majority only imagines its own tolerance."[14]

Blommaert and Verschueren above show that deriving an understanding of a written text is always a subjective exercise. Recent scholarly trends have sought to seriously challenge the notion that texts contain clear publicly-available information. Renowned hermeneutics expert Thiselton points us towards Derrida; "we have to turn to 'masters of suspicion,' the work, but not the world-views, of Nietzsche, Freud, Foucalt and Derrida

---

11. http://www.bucer.de/ressource/details/bonner-querschnitte-522015-ausgabe-388-eng.html.

12. Bhargava, "Rehabilitating Secularism," 101. See also Johnson, *First Step*, 94.

13. Masuzawa, *Invention of World*, 121.

14. Blommaert and Verschueren, *Debating Diversity*, 120. Blommaert and Verschueren's study uses a pragmatic approach to discern Belgium people's actual responses to immigrants, being quite different to the way the Belgian people like to portray themselves in public.

... in the struggle against manipulative interpretation."[15] Derrida's name is particularly associated with *deconstruction*.[16] In advocating deconstruction, Derrida wants to "expose and then to subvert the various binary oppositions that undergird our dominant ways of thinking."[17] Derrida seems to be on the same page as are we. "Nothing guarantees that another person will endow the words I use with the particular meaning that I attribute to them" according to Reynold's understanding of Derrida.[18] What then, according to Derrida, are the origins of the binaries that he is pointing us to? Here is the answer to that question given to us by Reynolds: "metaphysics affects the whole of philosophy from Plato onwards. Metaphysics creates dualistic oppositions and installs a hierarchy." We find also from Reynolds that "Derrida seems to be able to disavow any transcendental or ontological position."[19] Hence Derrida finds dualisms to be both very widespread, and ungrounded.

It seems to be strange for a Christian theologian to stand *with* Derrida. Hence Sweetman's critique of Derrida attempts to support Maritain's view that "the [human] intellect knows . . . reality as it really is."[20] On the contrary, Derrida considers that "*all identities, presences, predications etc., depend for their existence on something outside themselves, something which is absent and different from themselves.*"[21] Derrida is stating that the whole of human life is dependent on "*something outside[of us]*" (from above). How can a Christian argue with that?

Space prevents me from making a closer exploration of all the implications of post-modernism in this text. Derrida is one of the founders of post-structuralism already mentioned as instrumental in the founding of post-modernism above.[22, 23] I want to draw on at least two things that Derrida makes abundantly clear.

---

15. Thiselton, "Situating a Theoretical," 32.
16. Reynolds, "Jacques Derrida."
17. Ibid.
18. Ibid.
19. Ibid.
20. Sweetman, "Deconstruction," 234.
21. Ibid., 236. Italics in the original.
22. Derrida's is one of five names mentioned as key founders to contemporary post-structuralism .Williams, *Understanding Poststructuralism*, 1.
23. See also Harries, "African Development," and Harries, "Mission in a Post."

First is that binaries commonly used in western thinking and western philosophy are not "written into the order of things." These are the dualisms that I frequently refer to in this text. A very common error made by those intervening in majority world situations, is their tendency to presuppose that the local population thinks dualistically. Dualistic thinking, Derrida makes clear, originates in *ungrounded* ontologies. Because they appear to him to be "ungrounded," Derrida disavows them. These days so does, in theory at least, much of the West. Here is a gaping blunder which is daily being performed in front of our eyes; the western world clearly operates on foundational dualisms that originate in its metaphysical history, yet it denies the truth claims of that very metaphysics. Those truth claims are "grounded in" biblical writings. We are back to "kicking away the ladder." (See page 38.) I have talked above about the Bible being foundational, and of course foundational to the Bible being the early texts of the Bible, especially the Pentateuch in the authorship of which Moses is considered to have been influential.[24] When the legitimacy of a biblically-based foundation is accepted *by faith*, then everything else can fall into place. Denying such foundation is to put in place mechanisms that will have "everything else" collapse.[25] It is to undermine, in a sense, the ground we are standing on. We should thank Derrida for exposing "binary oppositions that undergird our dominant ways of thinking"[26] and hence come to realize that the West's metaphysical history is a part of who they are, denial of which is denial of its own foundations.

Second, I want to look at Reynold's suggestion that according to Derrida "nothing guarantees that another person will endow the words I use with the particular meaning that I attribute to them" (cited above). Without being able to consider the totality of hermeneutical innovations that have recently seemed to undermine some people's faith in the Bible, I suggest that the exposé of western metaphysical inconsistency fuelled by Derrida

---

24. I will not enter here into debates on the authorship of the Pentateuch. Suffice it to say that while some modern scholars deny Moses' authorship, parts of the Pentateuch itself strongly suggest that he indeed wrote it, or at least parts of it.

25. Reynolds points out that Derrida considers Plato to be the starting point for metaphysics affecting philosophy and creating dualistic oppositions. According to Justin Martyr (100–165AD), Plato drew on Moses (http://biblehub.com/library/justin/the_first_apology_of_justin/chapter_lix_platos_obligation_to_moses.htm). Velikovsky states: "later Greek philosophers regarded Plato as influenced by Mosaic teaching" (http://www.varchive.org/ce/orbit/plato.htm).

26. Reynolds, "Jacques Derrida," as above.

implies,[27] as above regarding dualisms, that faith in the God of the Bible is a prerequisite to a move to some kind of objectivity in the comprehension of texts. Therefore, to suppose that texts are "meaningless," or that meaning is only found in the reader (implying that God cannot speak to a reader through a text),[28] widespread post-modern assumptions, is for the Christian, misguided.[29]

The above discussion leads me to my examination of the Qur'an, the main foundational text for followers of the prophet Muhammad, these days commonly known as Muslims.[30] The "religion" of Islam has recently received a lot of attention by Westerners.[31] Despite it being misleading to consider Islam to be a "religion," Muslim people's history has roots in both Christianity and Judaism. Hence we can say: dualism (and the use of binaries in thinking) are not entirely foreign to them.

Recent decades and even centuries have seen a decline in the considered authority of written texts. This seems to have resulted in a strong negative reaction in parts of the West to, for example, citations from Christian Scriptures. It is as if you can "make them say whatever you want to." The ways in which people have used Scripture to do the latter, I agree, has indeed been a problem. But having undermined the related assertion by Derrida above, I want to say that "texts do speak." Yes, they can be interpreted in myriad ways, and their interpretation is often majorly influenced by the linguistic-cultural background of the reader.[32] But that is not to say that texts say nothing.

With respect to the Qur'an, given the above discussion and much ink spilt about issues of translation and context, I believe I am nevertheless justified in outlining my personal reactions to my reading of the Qur'an. These

---

27. I am not suggesting that Derrida himself was aware of this implication.

28. See for example Maier, *End of the Historical*, and Fish, *Is There a Text*.

29. Note also my suggestions above that to consider human beings as entirely on the "natural" side of the "natural versus supernatural" divide may be to fail to grasp the complex depth of human identity and functioning.

30. There are many more Islamic texts than just the Qur'an. My focus here is only on the Qur'an itself.

31. As pointed out above, a foundational error made by western scholars is to consider Islam to be a "religion" in the first place. The latter category (religion) in European languages having been derived from devoted Christianity, this error results in western people starting with the presupposition that Islam and Christianity are profoundly the same.

32. See Harries, "Is It Post-Modern."

reactions are indeed personal. I am sure that my long-stay in Africa also affects the ways in which I understand and interpret. In 2001, and again a few years later, I read through an English translation of the Qur'an, and a year or two later read through it again.[33] I here share my personal reaction to particularly the first reading. My impression, as I recall from memory, was that the Qur'an, as I could understand it in English translation, is a book that would provoke devoted readers to a life of violence and aggression. In my mind it was a book that should be prohibited, so provocative to violence is its content.

The examples below come from notes that I made to myself as I read the Qur'an in English in 2001. I am aware that according to Muslims the Qur'an should only be read in Arabic. Only the Arabic can be correctly interpreted.[34] What I present points to a subjective impact that the Qur'an in English had on me as a reader, given my background and life-context:[35] Verses that stood out as a result of my reading chapters of the Qur'an in English translation are as follows:[36] 98:6, Christians will go to hell. 33:64–66 + 22:17, Non-Muslims will go to hell. 60:1 + 58:22, Muslims are not to befriend non-Muslims. 55:39 + 7:46, People with black faces are dwellers of hell. 40:56, Anyone who disputes the Qur'an is a proud person. 9:123, Muslims should fight unbelievers who are near them. 9:84, Muslims should not stand at the grave of a non-Muslim. 9:29, Fight Christians and tax them. 9:5, Kill unbelievers whenever you find them. 5:51, Do not befriend Christians.

What might these observations imply if it is true that the foundations of what is these days widely valued as modern or secular life including democracy and liberalism, are Christian? The implications include that for followers of Muhammad, the foundations could be considered to be wrong. Such a conclusion seems to spell disaster for today's globalizing world. If many of the foundations of global cooperation are specifically Christian, then Muslims may well object to them. Muhammadans, those who are submitted to Allah (i.e., Muslims), are told that Christians are their enemy (see above). Given the fact that Islam has numerous followers world-wide, it can seem to some that the only hope for the future of the world is to deny the

33. Qur'an, *Translation of the Meanings*.
34. Sanneh, *Translating the Message*, 187.
35. Qur'an, *Translation of the Meanings*.
36. The terms I write are notes that I made to myself at the time. I do not claim them to be word-for-word quotes.

Christian origins of what the West today so much values, in the hope that Muslims will accept what is of value without rising up against its foundation: Christianity.

I hope my reader has by this point realized—the possibility that opposition to Christianity in today's world is significantly an outcome of efforts to not aggravate Muslims. Similarly, pushes for atheism and agnosticism may be little concerned about discerning the nature of truth, but much about wanting not to cause offense.[37] Occlusion of history from view has the same aim. History is being re-written "as if" God has no part to play in human lives. "We have become the victims of our own historiography" Siedentop tells us, and, he adds, "not simply at a professional academic level."[38] The newly constructed history arising is, unfortunately, a lie. While perhaps a well-intentioned effort at procuring global peace, it is failing. It has to fail—because its foundation is not solid. Not only is it failing but it is dangerous. It is dangerous at least partly because of the many scholars, never mind laymen, whom it is deceiving. As I have indicated elsewhere—it has caused some Westerners to reject the claims of faith in Christ in favor of atheism or agnosticism.[39] Part of the deception we have already looked at is the widespread teaching that there are many "religions" of which Christianity is merely one. Young people especially it seems, instead of being guided by the wisdom of their elders are being misled in droves. The liberals, we have discovered, who are dominating educational systems (see above), are seeking, albeit with good intentions, to perpetuate such state of affairs.

This absence of God, referred to by Appleby as "the marginalisation of religion" is a foundational cause of "fundamentalisms," including Islamic antagonism to the West.[40] The strategy of concealing one's Christianity to avoid irritating Muslims evidently, at the end of the day, seems not to work.

---

37. A monk in a monastery in a Middle Eastern country explained this same situation to me in a personal conversation held in March 2015. "Islam is a big problem. Atheism can undermine Islam in a way that Christianity cannot" he explained to me. That is to say, Islamic apologists are well informed on how to counter Christianity. Conversion to Christianity and promotion of Christianity to the Islamic population of Egypt are both illegal. Presumably advocacy of atheism is not illegal, at least not when practiced by Muslims themselves.

38. Siedentop, *Inventing the Individual*, 351.

39. See for example this outcome of recent research in the USA: http://www.theblaze.com/stories/2012/10/09/pew-20-of-americans-are-now-atheist-agnostic-or-unaffiliated-with-a-religion/.

40. Appleby, "Rethinking Fundamentalism," 230.

Fundamentalists see this as a "conspiracy."[41] Appleby expresses disappointment that much more attention has not been paid to The Fundamentalism Project, the results of which were published in 2003.[42]

A confusion arising from the co-identity of Christianity and Islam as both being "religions" ought to be clear. That is, that both are likely to get credit for each other's strong points, and the blame for each other's weak points. If Islam has a strength, then Christianity also being a "religion" like Islam, will get some credit for it. This means that if Islam has a weakness, such as its orientation (if I am right above) to "violence and aggression," then Christianity is likely to be painted with the same brush. Unfortunately for Christianity, given the general negative view of Islam in the West, its being seen as "one of a kind" with Islam (i.e., both are "religions") is likely to have had more of a negative impact than a positive impact. "The perception of profound conflict between secularism and religious belief has been re-awakened . . . [as a result of] acts of terrorism which invoke . . . the name of Islam."[43] Meanwhile the fact that liberalism and secularism have religious (i.e., Christian) roots remains "by no means widely understood."[44]

The Fundamentalism Project provides us with a prime example of how confusion between Christianity and Islam as both being "religions" has seriously denigrated the reputation of Christianity. Fundamentalism, that was once considered a Protestant phenomenon,[45] was extended over many years to include reference to Islam.[46] Marty tells us that "in April 1995 . . . about half of the [stories we found] had to do with various forms of Islam" and then he adds as a note: "in fact so consistent was this concentration that through all the seasons of The Fundamentalism Project the scholars . . . were sometimes seen as having created an Islamocentric concentration, or ideal type."[47] Appleby, published in 2011 so probably based on the back of further reflection, tells us that "the label [fundamentalism] continues to be applied most frequently to Islamic movements and parties, although it is

---

41. Ibid., 243.

42. Ibid., 229. For more details on The Fundamentalism Project see here: http://press.uchicago.edu/ucp/books/series/FP.html.

43. Siedentop, *Inventing the Individual*, 149.

44. Ibid., 349.

45. Marty and Appleby, "Conclusion," 816.

46. http://www.theatlantic.com/entertainment/archive/2015/06/the-origins-of-fundamentalism/397238/.

47. Marty, "Too Bad."

also used to describe Jewish, Hindu, Sikh, and Buddhist actors. *Christians are now treated with more nuance; it is less common to conflate fundamentalists and evangelicals*"[48] (my emphasis). On reading Appleby, he does not seem to treat Christian fundamentalism in any particularly different way despite this acknowledgement at the start of his article. Nevertheless, The Fundamentalism Project seems to have taken us full circle. It took a phenomenon that was being applied to Christians, extended it to "everybody," then found that sufficiently careful analysis meant that it could not apply to Christians, but does still apply to everyone else. In going through that full circle we could say that Christians, before they emerged on the other side, had been veritably dragged through the mud.

Going back to Siedentop above, this is particularly of interest to me for at least two reasons. One, the above idiosyncratic understanding of history is one that many African people perceive as being nonsensical. They therefore see straight through it. Accordingly, because African people generally don't "get" the objections that contemporary Westerners have to Christianity, it is not surprising that the church is growing by leaps and bounds in Africa.[49, 50] Unlike Westerners, African people who reject the gospel have not moved into a "secular" category. Even if they talk about secularism, they do not mean what Westerners mean by it. "'Secularism' can refer to . . . a whole range of . . . ideologies concerning 'religion' [and] . . . also refers to different normative ideological state projects . . . and to different models of differentiation of religion, ethics, morality, and law."[51] Luhrmann refers to much African Christianity as "never-secular Christianity."[52, 53] Anthropological research by Robbins et al. shows clearly that becoming Christian in never-secular communities can have a deeply profound and lasting impact on a population: "Christian conversion can lead to substantial changes to people's conceptualisations even of core domains of cultural understanding

---

48. Appleby, "Rethinking Fundamentalism," 225.

49. See especially Jenkins, *Next Christendom*, 2.

50. One could add that the gospel in many ways seems to speak very directly into the African worldview, and assists people in overcoming some adverse aspects of that worldview, that I considered above to be "a spiral of necessary-pragmatism."

51. Casanova, "Secular, Secularizations," 66.

52. Luhrmann, "Hyperreal God," 371.

53. I have noted above my discovering that when an African scholar in Nairobi mentioned "secularism" he was referring to the pre-Christian traditions of his people. See page 80.

such as that of selfhood, domains anthropologists sometimes imagine are rarely subject to such profound transformation."[54]

On the other hand, it seems increasingly, that African people are not in charge of their own destiny, or even of their own development. Bronkema helps us to realize just how widespread is the influence of outsiders on the African continent. The foreign aid industry is, according to Bronkema, playing a "massive role" in economies in Africa and other less developed contexts.[55] I agree with him. An increasing amount of Africa's formal agenda is being determined by outside bodies. Increasingly, Africa is being led by many of the institutions, people and scholars who operate from the dualistic perspective we are here critiquing. They are being led by institutions whose founding fathers are being forced to appropriate the deceit of secular origins that I have mentioned above. They are being led by a system of knowledge-discovery, scholarship, and academia that is rooted in Christ-denying liberalism. They are being led by the kind of people described by Green in his book that tells us how millions of people who might still have been alive are long-dead as a result of misguided liberal advice regarding sexual ethics.[56] They are being led, to use yet another terminology this time from Hof, by people who consider themselves correct by default and who are "invulnerable" in their approach to Africans.[57]

In the same vein Shaw tells us how the above tendencies have also affected missionary engagement. The influence of liberals on Christians has contributed to having the latter fail to see certain contextual dependencies of their message. As a result, interpretations of biblical texts achieved in the light of a certain context have been assumed to be innate to the text, as if they are context-less. Efforts at contextualizing the gospel have been in effect an attempt at communicating interpretations arrived in the light

---

54. Robbins et al., "Evangelical Conversion," 587. While the research carried out that drew these conclusions was in Amazonia and Melanesia, it would seem also to have relevance to other never-secular societies such as those in Africa. This research seems to have undermined previous assumptions made by anthropologists that Christian conversion tended to be "shallow" and not have deep or profound social impacts.

55. Bronkema, "Flying Blind?", 226.

56. Green, *Broken Promises*, 105.

57. Hof, "Towards a Theology." Hof outlines this argument in more detail in her PhD thesis here: Eleonora Hof, "Reimagining Mission in the Postcolonial Condition. A Theology of Vulnerability and Vocation at the Margins." Zoetermeer: Boekencentrum, 2016.

of one context into another context from which the same interpretations could not be derived. Shaw explains as follows:

> Taking its cue from Nida, the communication model for mission that prevailed during the second half of the twentieth century focused on clearly presenting the codes and ensuring that the message as decoded was the "closest natural equivalent." ... The model was extremely helpful in enabling missiologists to develop the concept of contextualization, ... however, the model was relatively static and product oriented: the goal was to present the Gospel properly, as understood in the West, in a new context and thereby enable people to have God's word in their environment so that they could be enriched by knowledge that those in the West had already acquired. Mission became a matter of knowledge transfer, and it remained embedded in an essentially colonial approach to communicating God's truth. By default, the meaning of what God has to say was viewed as bound to the text, in the possession of the communicator, rather than being relevant to the context where the receptor lived.[58]

I would not deign to suggest that "secular" people have nothing to offer. They may in some cases or even in many cases have much to offer. But they are missing something. Someone who gives you a whole car but no spark plugs would have done better to leave you with your ox cart. One could add that unfortunately in the majority world, research indicates that secular interventions are easily understood as being corrupt and introducing corruption.[59] The 1% the secularists may be missing is at the same time 100%—it is God in his power and his glory. It is increasingly clear that the West's development was founded on Christianity. I ask again as I have already in this book: has the West kicked away the ladder?

Perhaps I can illustrate what might be missing with reference to Hof. She tells us that "it is precisely in their vulnerability that humans turn towards the glory of God."[60] I suggest that this works both ways. In their vulnerability humans turn towards God, but this turning to God also reveals human vulnerability. People without God are very vulnerable. Yet as Hof points out to us "White talk" is to do with invulnerability. The talk of Westerners is often about power, about how things should be done, about confi-

---

58. Shaw, "Beyond Contextualization," 209. See also Gutt, "So-What Factor."

59. Gupta et al., "State, Corruption," 587, read in the light of Gupta, "Blurred Boundaries."

60. Hof, "Towards a Theology." Pre-publication version accessed.

dence, about knowledge that is objectively true providing a foundation for everything else, i.e., it is about confidence in dualism, or to use Fauconnier and Turner's term, in form rather than in meaning.[61] On its own terms the above can come across as very real, powerful, even competent, but before the glory of God it melts into the background. Let's take an example of a regular church service in the West. All that the West has and knows may be there: There may be highly educated people, computers running the visual and public address system, modern sophisticated cars bringing people to church, in democratic countries with stable governments and economies. Yet none of these should be the focus or purpose of people's being there. People ought to be in church to encounter God. Their nakedness is thus exposed. They are mortal flesh and blood liable to lose complete touch with all they have ever known at any time; that is, they could die at any moment. Hence they are incredibly vulnerable, bowing to a power greater than they. There, in universal human vulnerability, I suggest, is a thick connection cross-culturally with African people. Human vulnerability shows the potential for great things ahead. God meets such vulnerability with truth, in Christ, and then that truth can turn the world upside down!

The truth that can turn the world upside down, it should be noted, is not a formula, but a relationship. It is not love alone that will solve the world's problems if that love is separated from Christ. Neither does democracy exhaust the depths of Christian teaching. Certainly education does not do such. Christ is always more than these things.

It strikes me that African people are more aware of the God-dependent complexity of human life than are many Westerners. They have not been "fooled" by secular talk. It seems that this applies to everyone outside of the West. It is only the West that is "secular" in a western way.[62] Yet the West seems very certain that they are right. The rest of the world often agrees with them—many are, for example, struggling to get a western education. The reason, it seems clear, is because the West has indeed got something right. Secularism has much of the fruit of the gospel (the words of God presented through Jesus Christ). Yet I suggest that something is missing! The other reason the others consider the West to be "right" is because the West maintains a system of hegemony and domination of the rest of the world based on economic and military power, that obliges them to follow it.

---

61. Fauconnier and Turner, *Way We Think*, 3–7.
62. Taylor, "Western Secularity," 36.

One cause of the apparent invulnerability and inflexibility of the West seems to be its confidence in liberalism. Even those who might not themselves be atheists as such seem to accept that the world runs mechanically. Hence they see no need for God, as a result of which godly "vulnerabilities" as described above by Hof, do not arise. When there is godlessness, there can be no sacrificial love for others by God's servants on behalf of their father in heaven. Mutual faith in God has often unified otherwise disparate people. Such a route to peace-making has been "disallowed."

I do want to take some time at this point to look at atheism in the West in more detail, and especially at the reason for this incredible difference: on the one hand widespread atheism in Europe and elsewhere in the West, whereas it is difficult to find even one self-acclaimed atheist in sub-Saharan Africa.[63]

One sometimes hears the view shared, that African people are much less materialistic than are Westerners. That is to say—that they are less desirous of material wealth. I am inclined to dispute that. I think that the evidence supports my disputing it. I have observed that African people like to become wealthy, perhaps even more so than do Westerners. The major difference between Africans and Westerners is, I suggest, not in different levels of desire for wealth, but in their having different understandings of just how one should acquire such wealth. Luhrmann points to this when she tells us that although Ghanaian people in general may be relatively poor, some of their pastors become very wealthy.[64] Wealth is often acquired through what we could in the West call "spiritual means."

In short, African people are as desirous of material wealth as is everyone else, but they see the source of wealth and how to get it differently from Westerners. This should not be surprising in the light of prior discussions above. Westerners on the whole do not seek to acquire material wealth through spiritual avenues. They have already divided their understanding, between material and spiritual because they have a dualistic perspective. They seek for material wealth in the material realm. This makes African

---

63. While I suggest that it is difficult to find even one self-acclaimed atheist in Africa, that is only partly true. Many activities from the powerful West extend themselves to Africa. That is—western organizations often search for African partners, especially amongst English-speaking Africans with whom they can communicate relatively easily. Atheist organizations are surely no exception. Hence one should expect to find atheistic organizations in Africa modelled on those in the West. There is cause to think that some adherents to those organizations may be in it for the money.

64. Luhrmann, "Symposium Response," 232.

people's means of searching for wealth hard for Westerners to understand.[65] As a result, when African people's grasping for human flourishing happens in the form of the prosperity gospel, it is easy for Westerners to condemn it.[66]

The answer to the question of how one acquires wealth by spiritual means is a complex one. It falls outside of Westerners' radar screens, and beyond the range of western English. Describing it can also open one up to accusations of racism, as with respect to Africa one would seem to be identifying a trait (a tendency towards "superstition") amongst black people not found amongst many white people in the contemporary world. I borrow a few paragraphs from an as-yet unpublished article below:[67]

> Various commentators have noticed that a large amount of Jesus' teaching is about money and wealth.[68] Many of his parables concern this area of human economic living. Some may be surprised by this in this era, when Jesus' teachings are thought to be on the side of the 'spiritual' rather than the 'material'.
>
> Writings by the famous French anthropologist Marcel Mauss may help us to better understand Jesus by throwing new light on the nature of pre-modern economies.[69] Many western people seem to assume that material transactions were, before the advent of money, based on bartering, i.e., exchange of goods considered to have some equivalence in value. For example, if I rear goats and someone else grows cabbages then to bring variety into my diet I will exchange a goat for cabbages. Someone else gets a goat for a bag of maize, and so on. There is some truth in this conception of life-before-money, but it is not the whole truth.
>
> Mauss, looking at reports coming from different parts of the world, noticed a prominent practice of feasting and celebration amongst non-western people. Those celebrations did not involve calculated exchange value. Instead they seemed to be means of impressing others regarding one's own 'successes', as demonstrated in flagrant bountifulness in the giving of gifts, including food. The gifts were not repaid through barter exchange. Instead they set up

---

65. Maranz (in *African Friends*) has made a very gallant effort at describing it.
66. Such as Cotterell, *Prosperity Theology*.
67. Harries, "When God is Fortune."
68. For example, see http://jamesmirror.com/jesus/jesus-view-of-wealth/.
69. Mauss, *Category*. I say that Mauss throws "new light" on pre-modern economics. Of course what he actually does is throw "old-light," i.e., he reminds us of what was once presumably common or even universal understanding.

a certain obligation for return that was not in the material realm of calculation, but in the spiritual realm! Material generosity for these people set up levels of spiritual advantage over those who have not been generous. This spiritual advantage is by the Mauri[70] people called *hau*.[71] Amazingly, this term very much resembles a Luo term which seems to be equivalent, often spelt in Luoland as *hawi*. Amazingly again—this is the same *hawi* that we have considered above to be an equivalent to the English term fortune.

The link between 'good fortune' as per 'good luck' and fortune in the sense of great wealth is very evident in English; the same term fortune is used for both. Could it be that in English fortune (as per wealth) has also in the past been seen as arising from fortune (as per luck)? Fortune (i.e., *hawi*) seems to have a very material foundation for the Luo people of Kenya. In so far as *hawi* is God, then this means that God has a very material foundation. (Indeed, looking at the etymology of the English term fortune, we find it originates "from Latin Fortuna, the name of a goddess".[72])

Hawi and *hau* are mystical forces that bring prosperity. Their nature and shape arises from the nature and shape of material and economic transactions. Here we have an apparent integral relationship between the material and spiritual, that is very foreign to some recent strands of philosophy that have tended towards positivism. This positivistic philosophy has influenced even those Christian believers who have been nurtured and raised in the West. A part accommodation to positivism, seen as a kind of apologetic for Christian belief, has been incorporated into western Christianity. Hence some western Christians, especially evangelicals who can be said to be particularly a product of the modern era,[73] have drawn a clear line between spiritual and material causation, resulting in doctrines like that of cessationism.[74]

70. Modern spelling "Maori."

71. Mauss, *Category*.

72. http://www.oxfordreference.com/view/10.1093/oi/authority.20110803095829988.

73. "Evangelicalism came to regain focus and lighten the load" following the liberal (inspired by modernism) versus fundamentalist divide of the early parts of the twentieth century (http://www.reclaimingthemind.org/blog/2011/05/what-is-the-difference-between-and-evangelical-and-a-fundamentalist/).

74. "Cessationism is the view that the 'miracle gifts' of tongues and healing have ceased—that the end of the apostolic age brought about a cessation of the miracles associated with that age. Most cessationists believe that, while God can and still does perform miracles today, the Holy Spirit no longer uses individuals to perform miraculous signs" (http://www.gotquestions.org/cessationism.html). Are Cessationists right? Not according to christianchat.com: "We cannot deny that the supernatural gifts of the Spirit have at

If *hawi* arises, as it appears it does, as a product of pre-modern economic relationships, and the same *hawi* comes to be associated with God (or the Holy Spirit) in non-western churches, and also *hawi* can be translated as fortune, then the relationship between fortune and God is here evidenced. This presumably underlies the tendency for African Christians to be oriented to the prosperity gospel.[75]

This arises simply from their understanding of who God is: integrally associated with material prosperity. The relationship between God and fortune is not merely a linear one based on naivety. It is a complex one rooted in the nature of pre-modern ways of life that reflect human nature itself.

It is in this context that we can, I suggest, most helpfully consider Jesus' teachings on the nature of and our appropriate relationship to fortune. As the origins of this relationship are not simple, neither are Jesus' teachings about it.

I suggest it is not as simple as have been some positivists' views which consider fortune to arise from a non-relationship (aside from ways in which it can be rationally identified e.g. sexual morality will stop the spread of AIDS and venereal diseases). The art of unpacking Jesus' articulation of this relationship is really that of the preacher, prophetically inspired by God's Spirit.

The above paragraphs point to a severe gap in western ontology. Terms like fortune, chance, and luck seem (as a result of secularization, or the spread and dominance of science) in western ontology, to point to nowhere. English retains words such as luck, chance, and fortune but has redefined them in a way that seeks to make them compatible with science. Science itself has no answer for ultimate questions. Science is good for understanding how things happen, not why they happen. Why is left blank. That blank is large. The rest of the world is amazed and incredulous that a blank can just be left like that. Actually of course the "blank" is for the West implicitly filled by Christianity. As indicated above—this is one of the West's best kept secrets! We will see below that the actual picture is a little more complex than this. Yet, it remains true that the West conceals its

---

times diminished alarmingly. But without question we cannot deny that there are many verifiable incidents in church history that tell of the Holy Spirit's gifts being poured out, even in the darkest hours of church history" (http://christianchat.com/bible-discussion-forum/31047-does-church-history-support-cessationism-continuationism.html).

75. It would seem in some ways that the prosperity gospel is inevitable for people seeking a relationship with God, who do not clearly distinguish what is material from what is spiritual.

"soft underbelly," i.e., its long Christian history, during which time people believed very deeply and profoundly. Partly, as I suggested above, this is due to fear of offending adherents of Islam.

Africans do not have a blank in the "why" place. Although, frustratingly and confusingly they may appear to have a blank when they use English. This is one of the confusing shortfalls of use of such an "international" language. It does not rhyme with African worldviews. When Africans use it, Westerners easily get confused; it appears to portray Africans saying the kinds of things that Westerners believe.[76]

Within their own worldviews expressed in their own languages, the content of the "blank" left by Westerners dominates the lives of African people. They perceive prosperity, success, wealth, prestige, fame, happiness, fruitfulness, and so on to arise as a result of what we could in English call fortune, luck or chance—except as I have said above, the meanings of those terms have in English been re-appropriated. To understand Africa using English we would have to reinstate some of its more historical meanings. I will for my purposes here concentrate on the term fortune.

Clearly some people in the world are much more fortunate than others: one person dies perhaps at aged ten after a long and painful illness. Another will live to be ninety and will suffer almost no sickness until the day they die. Some people have happy marriages, intelligent and sensible children, inherited wealth, success in business, and the list goes on. Others acquire none of these things. Why do some people so prosper and others not? The answer seems to lie in what we are here calling their fortune, or the level of their fortune. Certain people are fortunate because they have good fortune, others are unfortunate because they have bad fortune. People searching for wealth and prosperity in Africa therefore tend to be occupied in searching for good fortune. Perhaps even more often—they seek to counter things that bring them bad fortune or that interfere with their good fortune.

The above searching for fortune in Africa does not run independently of African Christian theologies. It becomes incorporated into African people's understandings of God. That is to say—African people are not blank slates on which western theology can simply be written.[77] Instead, western theology written into African minds and hearts is transformed by the pro-

---

76. This is what Hiebert calls the flaw of the excluded middle. Hiebert, "Flaw of the Excluded."

77. Pinker, *Blank Slate*.

cess. This is why it is generally not appropriate to teach western (Christian) theology in Africa. The theology in, say, English, that is correct in the West, comes to be wrong in Africa.[78] Africans write *fortune* back into the western theology from which it has been removed. This disrupts, let us say, the *balance* of western theology.

Within African languages as within African understandings of English, God is not very distinct from fortune. It may even be that words whose meaning was really fortune have been used for translations of God in the Bible. I am not familiar with all African languages. I am familiar with Luo of Western Kenya. Luo has a set of terms that can indicate good fortune in the sense of mystical forces that make someone prosper. These terms include *Nyasaye, hawi* and *juok. Nyasaye* is the term most often used to translate God in the Luo Bible.[79] The two parts of the word *Nya* and *Saye* seem to indicate "the fruitfulness that comes from beseeching."[80] So then *Nyasaye* would be the one who, if one beseeches him, could provide fruitfulness. Furthermore, *Nyasaye*, is equated with *hawi*.[81] *Juok* is in contemporary Luo often translated as witchcraft, yet in the past, Hoehler-Fatton tells us, *juok* was considered to be good.[82] The Acholi people (who are closely related to the Kenya Luo) use the equivalent term *Jok* as the name for the supreme being, i.e., their translation for the English term God.[83] Mboya, a highly respected Luo author who catalogued Luo traditions[84] tells us that *Juok* is also called *Nyasaye*.[85]

Some, at least, Christian churches in Africa can be considered to be collective means of trying to bring fortune (in the old English sense of that term) to its members.[86] Unlike western Christians who tend to emphasize

---

78. Harries, *From Theory To Practice*, 1–20.

79. There are at least two translations of the Bible into the Luo language. I here refer to the 1976 translation.

80. Harries, "African Pentecostalism," 11.

81. Odaga, "Christianity and the African," 2.

82. Hoehler-Fatton, *Women of Fire*, xiv.

83. http://www.nalrc.indiana.edu/brochures/acholi.pdf.

84. Ogot, "Construction of Luo," 186.

85. Mboya, *Luo Kitgi*, 20.

86. They may do this in ways similar to Cargo Cults that became famous in the southern Pacific, whose people believed that "if the proper ceremonies were performed shipments of riches would be sent from some heavenly place" (http://www.sjsu.edu/faculty/watkins/cargocult.htm). (For "the authoritative account of the cargo phenomenon in New Guinea" see Lawrence, *Road Belong Cargo*, back cover.)

that they believe because they have been convicted about the truth of the Gospel, in my experience for many Africans the gospel would not make sense if it was not a means to prosperity. This ties in with Maranz' comment about inter-human relationships. Friendship that does not proffer some (material) reward makes no sense to Africans, Maranz tells us.[87] It seems to be very logical, that if the spiritual is not clearly distinguished from the material, as is the case for many African people, then the concept of receiving the spiritual without the material has no meaning.

Of course very often believing and following the gospel does bring African people prosperity. This is particularly often because western people support Christian groups with finance, but also in other ways.[88] Following guidelines of Christian living itself does bring certain kinds of and levels of prosperity. God blesses the people he loves.

We have found that for African people, seeking to be Christian is a means of searching for fortune. I now want to come back to secular people in the West, and to ask whether they are also seeking for fortune? In theory, we might say people in the West who use contemporary English *as defined in the dictionaries*[89] and who claim to be secular (even if they are also Christian) have meaningless lives. There is no meaning in pure science or objectivity. If they are simply basing all they do on science and objectivity, then perhaps we could say that they have no interest in fortune. Do they really live such science-based meaningless lives?[90]

I suggest that even so-called secular people who use contemporary English *are* also searching for *fortune*, in the sense that fortune is a means rooted in mystical forces that brings prosperity. This is demonstrated in diverse ways. For example, western people work with colleagues because they *feel* good about them. People do things in certain ways, thinking that a habitual way of doing them will help them to prosper. People consider

---

87. Maranz, *African Friends*, 65.

88. What have come to be in the Pacific area known as "cargo cults" are incredibly effective in much of Africa, if sometimes slightly more hidden. They have resulted in widespread rituals being performed in Africa, which are rewarded by donors from the West when they see Africans doing things that they consider to be important. For example, much practice in the educational system in Africa could be considered to be a cargo cult. This is not to be scorned. It can be very lucrative.

89. In practice many people do not use English in this way, i.e., they do address "why" questions.

90. We noted above that for all its appearance of secularism, 77% of Europeans claim to be Christian.

Fortune For Atheists

some colleagues to be lucky habitually—i.e., in a way that is beyond mere chance. People invest in the lottery. People play bingo. They say "touch wood." Someone can assure a friend "I will be thinking of you," imagining that their thoughts at a distance will somehow bring peace or prosperity to their colleague. People will follow hunches. Someone might toss a coin to help to make a decision. People wear black at funerals. Western people fear dead bodies. A fly landing in the soup might have someone throw away the whole bowlful. People find it disgusting to have a piece of chocolate shaped like a piece of poo. People value wearing an item of clothing once worn by a famous footballer. People go out of their way, perhaps at great expense, to be in the crowd welcoming a dignitary, the Queen or even the Pope to their community—even if they could just as well read their message in the newspaper the following day. People are friendly even to a stranger who they will never meet again. They will be friendly with this stranger even if the latter is about to die and no one else will know how they have behaved to him.[91] We could call these things superstitions.

We could be blunt and suggest that people who do any of the above acts yet claim to be secular are inadvertently lying. More helpfully perhaps would be to say that they are unaware of their actual dependency on mystical forces and powers. Why this lack of awareness? I guess one could propose many reasons. Shame? Because despite the fact that everyone "believes them," these acts are somehow (according to dominant western culture) illegitimate? It has become habitual to ignore them? They are part of a kind of underground-culture?[92] Or perhaps secular people and atheists openly hold to such beliefs, but they put them into a different category to "God"? Then someone will claim to not believe in god, while at the same time they practice what is mentioned in the above paragraph. They have defined "God" in a peculiar way that allows them not "to believe in him." Unlike widespread practice in Africa, they assume "god" to be somehow distinct from any derivation of fortune.

Let us portray the impact of Christian missionaries to Africa in a way that might help to get our point across. Let's take the native English practice of touching wood as a means of acquiring prosperity (or avoiding misfortune) as our example.[93] A wealthy western missionary could in some ways

---

91. A number of the examples given in this paragraph come from Rozin and Nemeroff, "Laws of Sympathetic."

92. This parallels ways in which people's belief in God can be "playful," see above.

93. Touching wood is said to bring luck. The origins of this particular belief are

be compared to an even wealthier-than-Westerners person coming to the UK or USA and telling people that touching wood is what can actually earn you thousands of pounds![94] Thus outsiders would have elevated the relatively low-level and low-key activity of *touching wood* to an entirely new status. This is comparable to the starting point of indigenous Christianity in Africa. Christian missionaries have taken an aspect of African "superstition," that is, fortune, and often used the vernacular term for it as the name for "God" in indigenous Bibles. What was an aspect of African superstition is elevated to enormous prominence. This is a route through which African people have learned about Yahweh, the God of the Bible.

Superstitions get played-down also in Africa. Though in Africa "superstitions" are perhaps more prolific and more determinative of a wider spread of life than in the West. African people do not have an indigenous alternative scientific explanatory system that occupies the territory occupied by science in the West.[95, 96] Instead a "superstitious" system of the acquisition of fortune is hegemonic. Certain parts and processes of the system have in recent centuries been appropriated by missionaries and Bible translators, so as to give diverse language groups in Africa an indigenous base for the articulation of Christian belief and theology. When viewed from this perspective, "secular" Westerners who believe in fortune[97] can be said, by using African Christian terminology translated back into English, to believe in god. In other words, either all traditional Africans are atheists, or there are no atheists. In other words again, according to certain prominent African conceptions of what it means to believe in God, all Europeans including secular atheists are believers. Gifford makes a parallel point: "the religion that two thirds of those living in poorer societies regard as 'very important' is often a totally different animal from the religion that four-fifths of those living in post-industrial societies regard as 'not important.'"[98]

---

apparently not clear: http://www.touchwoodforluck.com.au/history/.

94. As Robert Reese once pointed out (in *Roots and Remedies*, 63) a western missionary does not have to proclaim that they are telling people how to become wealthy. The incredibly high level of wealth held by the conversant compared to that of many people in Africa does that by default.

95. See also Horton, *Patterns of Thought*, 222, as discussed in chapter 5.

96. In so far as science is a part of a dualistic distinction, a holistic people cannot develop science. Mignolo, "Epistemic Disobedience," 9.

97. As defined in this chapter.

98. Gifford, *Christianity, Politics*, 164.

7

The Godly Way

SOME PEOPLE THINK THERE are ways of engaging others cross-culturally that are not rooted in God and his Word. Hence some Westerners come to engage with African people while denying faith in God. Some are even against faith in God. All this can seem amazing in Africa.[1]

The field of development sometimes attempts to ignore the impact of the gospel. I have heard practicing Christians say publicly that in development practice, they have a lot to learn from secular practice. Christian development initiatives can be modelled on non-Christian practice. This does amaze me. Not because we should not learn from one another, but because secular practices can miss the point. Jones illustrates this graphically in his recounting some of his research in a Ugandan village. "Projects" were here today, gone tomorrow, whereas the Pentecostal church in his village had become deeply integrated into local people's ways of life.[2] Jones is struck by the ordinariness of Pentecostalism in his earlier research in Teso, Uganda.[3] He seems to have expected the church to be isolated from village routine, for church members to be on "retreat from other local level Institutions,"[4] but instead finds them to be integrally involved in village and wider issues.

---

1. Part of the reason people think in this way is because they have narrowed their understanding of "God," as already discussed above.
2. Jones, "Making of Meaning," 75.
3. Jones, "Church in the Village," 513.
4. Ibid.

There has been a tendency "to side-line churches from the study of local level politics in the past," a tendency which should be rectified, says Jones.[5,6]

Part of the reason for the above types of confusion have already been alluded to above. Alternative views of history attempt to *deny* the Christian origins of the West's own development. Some perceive good reasons for rewriting history as if it is rooted in godlessness. Above we have discussed how such practices might originate in fear of Islam. Putting that aside, it seems to me that innovative development initiatives have always been rooted in godliness.

What I mention above are *not* small matters. In the 1991/2 academic year I completed a Masters degree in Rural Development at UEA (University of East Anglia): a major British university. The School of Development I attended had, as I recall, over one hundred post-graduate students. There must have been a few other confessing Christian students in our cohort. Perhaps one or two others had aspirations of working with the church in the majority world. The vast majority however, were anticipating working with secular bodies. I do recall a Christian colleague (from Japan) explaining that the above was because people were looking for salaried positions.[7] Their going for salaried positions was of course going to limit their innovative options; they were to be ruled by donors, boards, committees, red tape and other procedures of "a corporate worldview that panders to what investors want to hear."[8] I have lost touch I think with all of the above colleagues. They seem to live and work in a different world to mine. I do recall the above Christian Japanese student of development sharing that she would *prefer* to work in a church context, but frankly felt she had to go for a salary and career structure.

Some years later an Australian came to work in Kenya. She connected very closely to local people in my vicinity. A spell working with government initiatives in development in Papua New Guinea subsequently frustrated

---

5. Ibid.

6. Meagher (in "Trading on Faith," 400) similarly points out with reference to Nigeria how Christian institutions have become a key part of local African economic practice.

7. I was in the privileged position of already having by then a circle of churches and friends committed to standing behind me in my work in Africa, hence I was not obliged to look for a salary. That in itself seemed to be almost impossible to achieve outside of the church. My income from that circle of friends, however, was a lot lower than the then hoped-for earnings of my student colleagues.

8. Bessenecker, *Overturning Tables*, 180.

THE GODLY WAY

her no end after her grass-roots African experience, such that she resigned from the former.[9] Another colleague, in his late teens at the time, who was already being recognized as a gifted philosopher, came to Kenya thinking that it could be a good preparation for a possible career he had in mind of working in refugee camps in Africa. His perception of the difficulty of relating interculturally with indigenous Africans, who are free and independent in Western Kenya, put him off working in a refugee camp in which he as foreigner in charge would be yet much more set apart from the people. I take the above short case studies as demonstrating that others do "get" the advantages of a vulnerable Christian approach to intercultural engagement, as against heavy-handed (see more on this below) secular approaches.

I would like to suggest that the Bible provides *the* effective means of engaging cross-culturally in today's multicultural but globalizing world. Those who attempt to do "parallel things" to intercultural development assistance and globalized cooperation, by drawing on other than the biblical tradition, invite rounded criticism from today's global bodies. This is another way of saying that western secularism that guides global level bodies is, even though it does not acknowledge it, rooted in the Bible. An example of a means of intercultural and inter-ethnic co-operation that continues despite being widely condemned, and that is not rooted in the Bible, is the Indian caste system.[10]

I began to have this conviction that serving God is the premier avenue for intercultural service from around 1990, after I had lived for two years in Zambia. I have subsequently implemented the same conviction. That is, I have been seeking to serve God interculturally. Hence I will include a drawing on personal experience in my account below.

VISITING AN OLD MAN

On one occasion, after visiting an old man and ministering to him in prayer and with the word of God (from the Bible), I was convicted to write an account of that experience as part of an article for which I continue to look

---

9. This lady was not a professing Christian, but I would certainly argue that her approach was deeply rooted in Christianity, whether or not she would actually acknowledge that herself.

10. I rather suspect that my reader would think that terms like "intercultural and inter-ethnic co-operation" do not match with their knowledge of the caste system in India, which of course is my point. By comparison with the Indian caste system the much condemned apartheid of South Africa seems to have been very mild.

for a publisher.[11] The part of this article below illustrates how having a message about God can enable a cross-cultural approach that is not based on the provision of outside resources. It explains some advantages to such:

> Moving under the shade of the tree gave my sweaty body temporary relief from the scorching midday sun. Holding my bicycle in one hand, I greeted the young man with my free arm. We were standing alongside a mattress and some bedding material under the same tree outside of the man's mud thatched house in the heart of East Africa. While he was slashing grass, a woman was lying motionless, wrapped in this bedding on the ground. "*Ma chiegi*" (is that your wife) I asked? "*Kamano*" (indeed) he replied (all our conversations were in Luo). She was obviously very seriously sick. Wanting to visit the old man (the young man's father) first, I assured the young man that I would come back to him and his wife. As I moved forward, I noticed a lad of about seventeen years sat on a rock under another tree. I recognised him as the same lad with severe epilepsy that I had last visited a few years previously. He gesticulated with his arm as he struggled to speak. A few words came out. He pointed to the back of his father's house. The other brother had in fact already gone to call his father from the same place. A rather unkemptly dressed grey-haired man emerged and welcomed me into his abode. We sat. I knew the man was a widower. I knew also that he did not want to remarry but that he had devoted himself to looking after his severely disabled son.
>
> I already had an advantage in being fluent in the man's mother tongue (Luo) as well as in the regional language (Swahili). I had lived in the area for 19 years. Now as we sat in the dark unkempt sitting room end of his small square mud thatched hut, the question that loomed large was: what had I come to say or do? This poverty-stricken (certainly by British standards—my country of origin) old widower who constantly carried the burden of nurturing his seriously disabled son and was about to watch his only daughter-in-law die, living in a dirty compound in a mud house with a leaking roof, was sitting in front of me.
>
> The typical response from a Westerner would be something like—"I have, or I can give you access to, resources that will help you". On these lines my approach could have been to say:
>
> Have you tried this medicine for your daughter-in-law?
>
> Or—Make sure your daughter-in-law gets enough to drink. (Actually I did mention this. Water is usually a free resource!)

---

11. The working title for this article is: "Resource Use as Hindrance to Sustainable Overseas Development Intervention: A View Focused on Pentecostal Christianity."

Or—Let me take your son to hospital.

Or—Can I arrange for people to come to repair your roof?

Or—Why don't you try growing soya beans?

Or—Can I buy you a container for water to keep in your house?

Or—Why not keep chickens?

Or—Could you not take your son to a special school?

Or—I will lobby the government to help people like you.

Or—Take this money and take your daughter-in-law to a private hospital.

And so on. Each of the above approaches would be one that takes advantage of a superior access to resources on my part. I will not here go into detail about the many deep problems that this resource approach on the part of foreigners brings. For this I point my reader to Harries, "Immorality of Aid." My focus here is on the alternative options that this resource approach occludes.

Another approach I could have taken would be a *counselling* approach. I could have encouraged the old man to reveal all his problems as I *ummed* and *ahhed* my encouragements in response. Then I could have left him content in the knowledge that he had shared his burden with a careful listener. But what if, having heard about and perceived his burden, I wanted to share something more? Or what if, through my listening, I was actually implicitly legitimising something destructive? While Carl Rogers' approach to counselling certainly has its place even in Africa,[12] it tends to ignore the possibility that someone may be misguidedly directing their blame on supposed witches. Many people in Africa look for deep meanings and inter-personal causes for the misfortunes that overtake them. They perceive, for example, a relationship between their level of personal prosperity and any ill-feeling held by their family and neighbours. Some of these ideas about causation may be very personal. Others are held in common by communities. Ideas about certain behaviours leading to certain types of misfortune are codified in customary laws that prohibit the said behaviours. While often oral rather than written, these customary law codes are extremely complex (for an example of a set of laws that have been written down see Raringo, *Chike Jaduong*). The presence of such laws is no doubt widespread amongst human societies. Given their complexity, there is room for a lot of variety in ideas on how one's behaviour and that of others links to one's level of prosperity. People approach the prevention of misfortune from different angles. Many societies, if not all societies, have specialists

---

12. Saul Mcleod, "Carl Rogers." http://www.simplypsychology.org/carl-rog.

in means of avoiding misfortune (shamans, sages, priests, diviners and so on). The ideas themselves have an impact on the prosperity or otherwise of those who hold them. A set of ideas connected to witchcraft beliefs would be a good example of this. Misfortune being ascribed to another's ill feelings requiring revenge even on someone who is not (in a Western sense) directly responsible and even may not be aware that others consider them responsible for particular misfortune, as is the case in witchcraft beliefs, is a very widespread and destructive inter-personal dynamic.

Sitting in the old man's house, I was very aware of the above witchcraft beliefs. Had I had resources, I would have been able to attempt to sidestep such dominant belief systems (implicit law codes) by providing a resource-means of compensating for any perceived damage caused by witchcraft. Now what to do if I do not have resources available? (In the Alliance for Vulnerable Mission we suggest that some missionaries and development workers *not* access outside resources in certain key relationships. See vulnerablemission.org.)

The question that looms large is not *whether* I will engage with the mass of presuppositions about causation that this man is deeply aware of, but *how* I will engage with them. The above counselling practice—merely saying *hmm* if he tells me that he considers Mr or Mrs X to be killing his daughter-in-law by witchcraft, would be encouraging an unhelpful fear. Do I have anything to say to the old man? If I do not have why am I there in the first place? Am I there to gawp, or to bewitch someone, or to glean information for purposes of gossip, or just to have pity on the poor old fellow? A problem with many approaches to Third World development is that they have nothing to share that does not relate to or require outside resources.

If I am going to make such visits without the purpose of handing out resources (and dependence creation, and all the other problems that result from outside aid (see Moyo, *Dead Aid*.) then clearly I will need an ontology that will enable me to do this. I need to avoid, at least in this negative view, making myself simply an actor in a possibly very destructive drama going on in the heads of villagers. It so happens that I do have such an ontology—it is called the gospel of Jesus Christ. I do have something to say, and I have the Scripture as authority to say it. I had a copy of the Christian Scripture in the Luo language in my hands. As a result I was able to encourage the old man by pointing him to others whose faithfulness to God had seen them through difficulties. My interpretation of his difficulties was that God can allow trials to come even to the children whom he loves. I did have something to say to the disabled brother that was not a platitude: I read a portion of Scripture that related how Christ had given himself for others. I trust that he understood something, or at least appreciated my effort at communicating with him. I did have something to say to the very sick woman. I knelt beside her and held her hand, with the father-in-law and husband standing behind me, as I appealed to God on her behalf to take note of her case. I was able to give her hope for recovery that was not the identification of a witch; by recounting from Scripture how Jesus had healed Peter's mother-in-law (Luke 4:38–9). I was able to reduce the terror of death in this poor woman by telling her that God desired to live in her and that he had a plan for her for eternity!

Contrary to western thinkers whose menu of possibilities are restricted by materialist assumptions which have of late been very dominant on the scene of western interventions into the poor world,[13] I had a mass of options open to me! Those options were not simple. I needed to engage in prayerful and understanding thought: given this woman, or old man, and handicapped son, and their circumstances, how should I speak and what should I say? This can be considered in two ways. First, from the point of view of need. In the case of the lady, to enable me to do this I needed an understanding of what was in her mind as she faced this life-threatening calamity. Second, in order to have something to say, I had to draw on an ontology. Drawing on a private ontology would have meant I was really no more than a quack. I needed to use an ontology that was known, shared by others, had clear boundaries, a long history, numerous heroic figures, and an absolute truth claim. I had to prayerfully engage my understanding of God, of Christ, of the Scriptures, of the history of the church, with this woman's predicament, so as to carefully choose the Luo terms to use and the Scripture to read that made me into a part of God's plan for her life. I left her, I trust, more optimistic, more encouraged, more empowered, more at peace and closer to Christ than I found her (and the others at the homestead the same). The way they all heartily and warmly encouraged me to come again indicated that indeed I had done this—or rather that God had done it through me.

---

13. Interventions which focus on material aid of late have been very dominant on the scene of western interventions into the poor world. Martin Wolf, "Martin Wolf: How to help Africa escape poverty trap." http://www.ft.com/cms/s/1/d28aa0cc-6405-11d9-boed-00000e2511c8.html#axzz2ijRzZdMG (accessed October 25, 2013).

I want to consider a further side effect of my above activity. That is: my presence, actions and words had added to and changed the perceived ontology of that community in whatever small way (in terms of all Christians and all churches in that community accumulatively in a much larger way). I had reduced those people's fear of witchcraft. I had done so without leaving a physical resource to show for my presence. In fact, I believe my impact was the better for not having been connected to a physical resource, as the latter would have been generating dependency. Some may want to ask: was my impact consequential? Could I have been wasting my time? Does a community's ontology actually matter? Or, as suggested by Professor Jeffrey Sachs, are not ontologies changed by material inputs and not the other way around?[14] I will respond to Sachs below. Regarding the other points, yes, I did have an impact. It was easy to see how that impact was for good, even as Sachs may recognise *good*. The encounter had an impact also on me—on my heart and soul. It was an impact to good: it was an impact that revealed something of the truth of God. It was an impact that lifted people's spirits.

It was the gospel that enabled me to take an interest in the old man in a way not rooted in provision of resources or personal superiority. Thus it was really the gospel that enabled engagement that did not create outside dependency. It was the gospel that gave me a reason to visit the old man in *my* poverty. That is, other reasons for making the visit would have been creating dependency on outside aid. They would have been limited to times when resources were available. They would mean that my visits would have always been for another purpose. Visiting someone with the sole purpose of sharing encouragement from the Bible is demonstrating a profound concern for their soul. Such a visit creates a foundation for ongoing relationship that can weather many storms. Christian love should go beyond sharing resources. It is about eternity. It is a wonderful foundation on which to build intercultural relationships. In a sense it provides the foundation for intercultural relationships. If that foundation is lost, and reaching out to people of a vastly different way of life is reduced to being a means of simply sharing from a position of superiority to those who are inferior or vulnerable, then something precious has been lost.

---

14. Hoksbergen et al., "International Development," 21.

THE GODLY WAY

CAN YOU BE TRUSTED?

I once had a conversation with some anthropologists about ethics. We were discussing whether anthropologists have a moral or ethical stand. Related to that—do they attempt to or claim to pass on a moral message to the people they are reaching? I was told that morality is not of concern to anthropologists. Certainly they do not aim to pass on a message of a particular morality to the people they are seeking to research. Many anthropologists seem to take pride in having such a stand (or no stand, however one happens to look at it). On the other hand; how can the particular people "being researched" trust an anthropologist if that anthropologist refuses to be bound by particular ethical guidelines? Even if some anthropologists prove trustworthy, can they trust others who come with them or come later? Can they trust the anthropologist not to seduce their girls or to make them pregnant? I have personally heard anthropologists tell stories of having slept with local girls; it seems that no they cannot. As with anthropologists, so presumably with other development workers who go from the West to Africa and other parts of the majority world. The latter typically are not bound by particular sexual ethics. On the contrary—some may be gung-ho in favour of sexual freedoms.[15]

Anthropologists set out to observe rather than to change people's behaviors. Development workers usually intend to change behavior in particular predetermined specified ways. Both of these groups may therefore come under Lewis' category of "men without chests."[16] They do not intend to have a holistic impact. I would ask however—is moral neutrality even possible? I can certainly imagine young men in a community who might have been denied access to alcohol, being encouraged to rebel against such denial by the presence of an equally young visiting anthropologist who drinks as much as he likes when he likes. In many communities, morality is upheld using taboos backed by threats of misfortune. Such may be the basis for the upholding sexual morality. Having an apparently wealthy and prosperous anthropologist or development worker who at the same time is morally loose in one's midst, could prove a major incentive for young people to ignore their elders' advice on sexual morality.[17] The above does

---

15. Those people determining policy regarding AIDS prevention in Africa were, according to Green, totally opposed as a matter of principle, to restrictions on sexual freedom (in Green, *Broken Promises*, 39 and 66).

16. Lewis, *Abolition of Man*, 34.

17. Sexual misbehavior may well need to be regulated by prohibitions based on

not even touch on morality with respect to personal property (theft), truth telling, deception, illness, and debauchery in general. Slack foundations of morality may help to explain why anthropologists can end up unpopular.[18] The same presumably applies to secular "development workers." The latter may "compensate" for their immorality by providing funds, although to many that would be a poor compensation. Here is a quote from Winter, drawing on missionary experience in Guatamala:[19]

> Anthropologists are often possessed of the idea that culture is completely relative, so it does not matter how you act. Mountain villages had seen anthropologists whisk in for a few weeks and go out again, leaving behind a reputation of totally immoral behaviour. Missionaries, by contrast, came and stayed—for years on end—and were accorded the very highest respect.

Of course not all anthropologists are condemned as "totally immoral," and Christian missionaries are not faultless or immune to moral failure or laxity. Yet, few would doubt that missionaries do openly proclaim a clear moral stand, while anthropologists as a professional group do not necessarily do so. Extramarital sex, for example, is in Christian missionary communities roundly condemned. Use of alcohol is seriously curtailed if not outlawed. Christian missionaries have a holistic aim. They seek to represent a just and loving god and to convince others to follow their example. Their aim is to give a holistic witness to a community, and not just either to research them, or to "help" them using outside knowledge or resources. The moral stand of Christian missionaries seems to me to put them in a different league to secular efforts at intercultural engagement. Communities can learn to trust Christian missionaries in ways they never can others from the West.[20] Winter goes so far as to say, following his experience in Guatemala: "If I were in a mountain town and needed some cash, as a missionary I could write a simple IOU on a scrap of paper and borrow five dollars from anyone, believer or not."[21]

---

taboo because of the sensitivity and long-term nature of the issues involved. In other words, promiscuity can be pleasant in the short term, but very damaging in the long term.

18. Winter, *Frontiers in Mission*, 44.
19. Ibid.
20. As I mentioned above, there is no guarantee that they will be trusted, but there is I think clearly a higher likelihood that they will be trusted.
21. Winter, *Frontiers in Mission*, 44.

MATTERS OF THE HEART

Much ink has been spilt in discussing foundational causes of poverty and human deprivation. There are some who would give the cause of poverty in Africa as being a lack of capital. Perhaps Geoffrey Sachs would be one of those, saying as he does that "the vast barriers to development in Africa are not in the mind but in the soils, the mosquitoes, the vast distances over difficult terrain, the unsteady rainfall."[22] Dambisa Moyo on the other hand looks on the constant provision of capital to Africa to be a source of its problems rather than a solution. Referring to aid to Africa, she tells us: "these billions that have hampered, stifled and retarded Africa's development. . . ."[23] People's fear of being accused of being racist probably contributes to their favouring "lack of capital" explanations for Africa's poor showing on many development indicators.[24] In reality though it has been my observation that many, certainly those who have spent significant periods on the ground in Africa and who have got close to the people, realize that heart-issues contribute to poverty. That is—there are beliefs and certain stands taken by African people in their approaches to life that result in a lifestyle assessed by the West as poverty-stricken and undesirable.

If I am correct, as I believe I am in the paragraph above, then the means to a solution to poverty is not primarily foreign money, but a transformed heart. Here I would say that it is people who put the human heart at the cutting edge of their interventionist strategies who have the greatest hope of being able to "end poverty" in Africa. People who do that, classically, are Christian missionaries. Many believe a cutting edge guide to what mission work ought to be is found in Matt 28:19 which tells us to "make disciples of all nations" (NIV). The term disciples is close to the term "students." Christian missionaries aim to make people into students of Jesus. In a broader sense, students of the Bible and students of the church. Jesus is concerned with the heart of man. Such then is, or should be, the concern of Christian missionaries. What does a Christian missionary hope to transform the human heart into, may be the obvious question that follows here.

---

22. Sachs, "End of the World."

23. Moyo, *Dead Aid*, 9.

24. If the problem in Africa is lack of capital, then people are innocent victims of their circumstances. If one perceives poverty as arising out of certain behavioral/cultural traits, then one might seem to be taking a racist stand. I have looked into such links to racism in much more detail in another article, as yet unpublished (in Harries, "Anti-Racist Strategies").

The full answer goes beyond the bounds of this book. Perhaps in brief one could say: to be more like God (i.e., Yahweh). The task of bringing about such transformation is more than can ever be achieved by mere teaching. It requires a movement into communication with and relationship with the living God.[25]

The notion that what Africa "needs" in order to relieve poverty is outside funds has been prominent since the 1950s.[26] Although it is gradually being undone, its undoing has been rendered complex by an apparent lack of alternative solutions. The reason for such apparent lack is something I point to in this book. Intellectual fashions of our day have occluded an alternative solution from view (see above). It is about God. Continuing to deny God's role might (and certainly should) increasingly be seen as cruel perpetuation of global poverty. An alternative means of resolving poverty these days popular, is by enabling peoples who have been influenced by centuries of western Christianity (i.e., Westerners) to control more and more of what goes on in Africa. Unfortunately this causes masses of unhealthy dependency. Williams accuses the West in the following stark terms of:

> systematically destabilising the wealthiest African nations and their systems, and all that backed by huge PR campaigns leaving the entire world under the impression that Africa is poor and dying and merely surviving on the mercy of the West. Well done Oxfam, UNICEF, Red Cross, Life Aid and all the other organisations that continuously run multi-million-dollar advertisement campaigns depicting charity-porn to sustain that image of Africa globally. Ad campaigns paid for by innocent people . . . [Williams suggests on the contrary that Westerners] should come [to Africa] *empty handed* filled with integrity and honour . . . (my emphasis).[27]

"The meek . . . will inherit the earth" says Jesus, in Matt 5:5. This passage in Matthew's Gospel has, I believe, vexed many Christian believers. Hence in English I have personally often heard it said that "meek is not weak." The English term meek seems to suggest weakness. In Greek usage the term πραεῖς, that is translated into English as meek, is used to refer

---

25. My reader may well note a radical clash here with Islam, were this paragraph to be taken seriously, further emphasizing my case in this book that fear of Islam has caused people to hamstring Christian mission.

26. Moyo, *Dead Aid*, 13.

27. Williams, Pillage des Ressources.

to a horse that has been broken in.[28] A horse that has been broken in can be useful in a way that a wild horse can never be; it can be harnessed for various tasks, such as pulling a cart, or transporting a person. A wild horse is of no value to a human community, except perhaps for its meat. A horse that has been broken in can be of great value and can perform many useful roles. I suggest that this is a helpful way of understanding meekness. Meekness is "power under control."[29] My mind goes to *Champion the Wonder Horse*, which we used to see on TV when I was a child. Champion was a very strong and very bold horse, but all that would have been to no avail to 12-year-old Ricky had he not also been willing to respond to people's needs.[30]

Champion the Wonder Horse of course had no money. The value of a broken-in horse is not in the money that the horse has access to. I believe this tells us something of the meek who will inherit the earth (Matt 5:5). It can seem surprising, and this is the contrast that Jesus presumably intended for us to pull us up short, that someone without money could end up inheriting the earth. There is great irony and apparent contradiction in this. Most people who want to "make a difference" to improve other people's lives or eradicate poverty probably have quite early on to be thinking "where might the necessary money come from?" Jesus is making a point—inheritance of the earth as here expressed is not a matter of wealth.

I believe there are some profound things to be learned here about the approach to Africa that can bring effective transformation. That approach must not be money. Because "money makes the world go around," as they say, to state this is (yet again) to enter into apparent contradictions: if everything runs by money, then how can one end poverty or work effectively for Africa by means that are not money?

Perhaps it is helpful to reverse the above and ask ourselves how one could use money to help Africa. Money is a relative newcomer to Africa. Until recent centuries, many of its people got by entirely without it. African people are not familiar with its use at depth. Let's say that African culture left to its own devices does not produce money. This means that interventionary practices that are foundationally built on money set an example that local people cannot imitate. As mentioned above, they are also liable

---

28. http://www.basictraining.org/print.php?nid=216.
29. Ibid.
30. http://www.imdb.com/title/tt0047703/plotsummary?ref_=tt_ov_pl.

to become a means of corruption, or to encourage that which is considered to be corruption.[31]

We could look at Jesus' example to build on the above paragraph. The Bible records no incidence of Jesus providing funds in order to continue his ministry. Apparent exceptions may include finding the coin in the mouth of a fish (Matt 17:27) and feeding crowds of thousands (John 6). These exceptions though prove the rule—in one instance Jesus *found* the money that he was to use in the mouth of a fish. When he fed thousands, food was obtained without use of money. Jesus did not withdraw money for it from an account or a treasury. That is not to say that funds were never used, or that money was off the radar screen. On the contrary, Jesus often talked about money. Yet consistently his ministry, as communicated for us in the gospels, was not carried out through money. He is not depicted as giving handouts or as being occupied in raising funds.

I believe the above to be a vital component to the instigation of sustainable development in Africa. This for at least one further reason: by putting himself in a position of having no money, a missionary (i.e., a Westerner living and working in Africa) is identifying with the foundational position in which Africans find themselves. As he so identifies with them, then by default, any way out of poverty that he advocates will, all other things being equal, be one that local people can imitate. Here we are getting an apparently counter-intuitive but key principle for intercultural intervention directly from the Bible, God's book.

It needs to be added that there is a condition which qualifies the above. That is, that the outsider who is wanting to work without access to outside resources must engage using local languages. Use of outside languages severely limits comprehension at depth, and very soon brings misunderstanding.[32] An ability at local languages is essential in order to grasp what is going on, and in order to be "within reach" of people wanting to provide helpful correctives to the way one is living and working.

---

31. All of the above is not to try to deny African countries the "advantages" of a money economy. It is simply to help a Westerner wanting to contribute to human flourishing in Africa to know how to do so.

32. Of course use of non-local languages is also problematic for those who do bring in resources.

The Godly Way

PRAYER THE SOLUTION

Solutions can appear simple until one knows the extent and complexity of a problem. Hence other people's marriage problems can seem as if they ought to be easily resolved, while one's own might seem unfathomable. Hence the West's own issues can seem intractable. Looking out into the majority world, Westerners see the kinds of problems that they have already solved, sometimes some generations ago. Westerners perceive Africa as being where they once were. Westerners may well see themselves having a lot to say to help Africa to progress, if only they would listen.

Often Africa appears to be listening. I say "appears to be" because listening can mean different things. Not everyone shares the West's bluntness in "calling a spade a spade." Other people are more fearful of confrontation. They would rather say no through their action when you are not there, than to your face in your presence. I think this is a very hard lesson for Westerners to learn. It raises basic questions of truth in intercultural communication.

When truth (as this term is used in the West) cannot be known with certainty, intervention in the traditional sense may not be advised. Take an instance in which a wife has fled from her husband. She may be looking for someone to support her so that she can live independently of her family. Should a missionary/donor provide her with that support? If they do, that may keep her from going back to her husband. The husband might want her back. Deep in her heart she may want to go back. She may even want to need to have to go back. The provision of support has interfered with the re-unification of a married couple. Take another instance, one that I met recently. A church plant appears to have failed. No one was worshipping on the Sunday, and the pastor had opened a café-business in a nearby village. The café was open on the Sunday. On talking to him, he explained that the government had closed the church because he did not have a title deed for the plot on which it was built; the land was still in the name of his grandfather. To get a title deed for the church ground he would need to go to the government to get the land first into the name of his late father, then to divide it up into the names of the sons, then he as one of the sons could give the land for building of the church. That process, I was told, would take up to $1000.00 to expedite. It would seem that a major financial donation from the outside could be justified because it *might* rescue the church plant? On the other hand—it is my suspicion that other factors, especially internal divisions, that have actually crippled the church. If the pastor is sufficiently dedicated to Christ, then why has he opened a café and is he selling tea there on a Sunday morning? Provision of the money may well not rescue the church plant, but it could produce a lot of jealousy and infighting. Prayer to God however does not have that problem. The challenge to the person aware of this situation might be; do I have sufficient faith to pray? That is a healthy challenge.

A missionary colleague of mine here in Kenya has clearly picked up this baton. Recently a bus in which I was travelling in Kisumu in Kenya stopped for some passengers to alight and board at the gate to a large government hospital. As we were stopped I saw a missionary colleague of mine standing just a few yards away surrounded by a group of local boys. I called to one of the boys to nudge him to look my way and see me. We greeted one another. I asked him what he was doing there. "Going with the boys to pray for cancer patients" he told me. I was caused to reflect on his words. It is hard to transform the medical practice in a large government hospital in Kenya. Often what goes on is very different to western medical standards. People do not always like to be told what to do or what not to do, especially by foreigners who think they know better. Going into an African hospital as a foreigner to tell workers to "pull up their socks" could get acrimonious. The foreigner could find himself isolated or jettisoned! On the other hand, and this is what my friend seemed to have realized—people are unlikely to be upset by prayer ministry. They might even be encouraged by it. Corrupt elements more interested in making money than in the provision of a healing service may be challenged by it. Prayer can be a powerful ministry and witness, that does not directly confront, and so will not raise opposition from political players in the system![33]

Prayer is helpful in contexts, like hospitals and other institutions, where there may be intense competition over resources. Prayer can also be helpful in other complex situations in which it can be hard to know how to help a person. Giving out resources is usually fraught; it is very difficult to do so impartially. Unless one's resources are endless (which is unlikely) in African contexts of widespread great need, resource distribution causes disputes, splits, and fights.[34] Prayer much less so. Resources may not help

33. This is of course related to Jesus telling Pilate that "My kingdom is not of this world" as per John 18:36. Financial assistance invariably requires some kind of accountability, which means some kind of control, which can easily be resented.

34. Frank Paul shared with me how similarly, in Argentina in their ministry with indigenous Indians he was told "you make that we don't fight within our communities/churches" (personal communication, December 2015). This is in contrast with people

or may only barely help in certain situations. Prayers really are always appreciated.[35]

THE MAN OF GOD AND THE WITCHDOCTOR

The identity of a "man of God" in Africa does not arise out of a vacuum. It arises out of people's prior knowledge. "Every people has its history, its way of coping with reality, and that any new concept that comes to them is received and interpreted in terms of all the experience this people has had up to that moment, and that it is impossible that they respond to God in any other way that is not their own" Buckwalter had learned.[36] In the case of the Luo of Kenya, I have already shared something of their foundational understanding of God. A traditional name for God (god) has been *juok*.[37] The Luo people also have specialists who, based on their knowledge of "god," are able to help people. These traditional specialists are known as *ajuoga* (plural *ajuoke*). *Ajuoga* can be translated into English as doctor. More often though, it is translated as witchdoctor, *juok* being witchcraft.[38] The base-identity of a man of God is therefore in many ways rooted in the role known in English as the witchdoctor.[39] The witchdoctor seeks to use his/her superior knowledge of god to assist people, especially those going through problems or difficulties.

Note that in Africa, unlike in contemporary Europe, there is no tradition of the use of science to resolve social or relational issues. Disciplines that attempt to do so in Europe, such as psychology, psychiatry, etc., are

---

who do relate to people in indigenous communities with resources that can end up causing people to fight one another for those resources.

35. Someone might here point to James 1:17: "faith . . . if it is not accompanied by action, is dead." While this is true, I would point out that sometimes action is difficult, or options for action are more limited, and of course that prayer is itself an "action."

36. Buckwalter and Buckwalter, "Mission to the Indigenous," 158.

37. See chapter 5. Inventing Godlessness Amongst Christians, page 60.

38. A literal translation could be something like "only witchcraft."

39. "They helped us to understand that every people has its history, its way of coping with reality, and that any new concept that comes to them is received and interpreted in terms of all the experience this people has had up to that moment, and that it is impossible that they respond to God in any other way that is not their own" said Buckwalter in 1987, some years after Dr William Reyburn had advised the Mennonite missionary force in the Argentina Chaco to change their missionary strategy. Buckwalter and Buckwalter, "Inculturation of the Gospel," 158. Hence people are bound to respond to God's word from the basis of their own prior understandings.

strangers in Africa. That is to say that people are accustomed to seeing their help come from god/God/gods. This gives a God-believing missionary a slot to use to fill a space in African culture, which a secularist does not share. The above is to say, in other words, that many African people traditionally see the means for resolution of their problems to be some kind of shifting of or manipulation of mystical powers.[40] We have mentioned above that Christians are interested in making *disciples* of Jesus. The term disciples in the New Testament (μαθητής) can be translated into English as students. Someone becoming a disciple is therefore putting themselves into a learning position. Educational theorists tell us that effective education goes from known to unknown.[41] Thus Christian discipleship should take someone from their (taken as) faulted understanding of God to a "correct" understanding of God. This is how a change agent who is to bring sustainable indigenously-rooted change to Africa needs to operate. That is to say—he will work on and with faith in God, beginning with where people are in their pre-existing comprehension of god. God is required.

IMPARTING INNOVATIVENESS

I notice that courses on entrepreneurship are of late being offered here in Kenya.[42] This is an essentially outside-instigated foreign-funded initiative designed to fill a perceived lack or shortfall in Kenyan/Africa communities. Unfortunately, as normal, and contrary to the principle I have mentioned above whereby education should go from known to unknown, curricula for teaching entrepreneurship, together with the language of instruction, all come from the West.

Westerners generally consider themselves to be capable of innovativeness and its close cousin entrepreneurship. They consider Africans to fall short in this area. This raises the question of how to encourage these qualities in Africa?

I would like to agree with Mangalwadi that most of the innovativeness that has in recent centuries erupted in Europe has done so on the back of the Bible.[43, 44] Mangalwadi tells us that "Education was a Christian mis-

40. Kasomo, *Belief in Mystical*.
41. http://www.beesburg.com/edtools/glossary.html.
42. Rori et al., "Revitalizing Youth," 123.
43. Mangalwadi, *Book That Made*.
44. I use the term "innovativeness" to mean something like "lateral thinking." I

sionary enterprise. It was integral to Christian missions because modern education is a fruit of the Bible. The biblical reformation, born in European universities, took education out of the cloister and spread it around the globe."[45] "Technological innovation . . . took place in Christian monasteries, whereas science grew in Christian universities" Mangalwadi tells us.[46] Prah agrees that it was Protestantism that succeeded in un-bottling the reproduction of knowledge from the hands of "narrowly based religious . . . elites."[47] The Christian faith has been and still is a springboard for education, and for encouraging innovation. Possible reasons for this are many, including:

1. It presents truth, and truth sets people free from error.

2. It presents knowledge of God the creator of heaven and earth. Knowledge of the creator is a means of improving one's understanding of the creation.

3. Jesus' death on the cross can lift people above and clear of numerous pitfalls of tradition and taboo that otherwise tie people hand and foot. It was Christian Puritanism that, unintentionally, resulted according to Weber in wealth-generating innovativeness.[48]

4. The Christian faith frees people into a supportive system of morality. It is not a discarding of laws, customs and traditions so much as their fulfilment (Matt 5:17). Thus it produces order and not chaos, relationship rather than antagonism.

5. The Christian faith is not "tied and done." In that sense, it is democracy and not dictatorship. Dictatorship tries to suppress discussion. Democracy encourages its expression and extension. You could say—Christianity is a guidebook rather than a rulebook, yet it displaces and replaces rulebooks.[49]

---

concede that this is a culturally-loaded term, which is the point that I am making. I do not have the space to unpack the complex theology that underlies what in the West are known as "innovation" and "education."

45. Mangalwadi, *Book That Made*, 194.
46. Ibid., 100.
47. Prah, "Introduction: Winning Souls," 5.
48. Bendix, *Max Weber*, 139–40.
49. The kind of "rule book" it displaces here in Kenya is illustrated by Raringo in *Chike Jaduong*. Most African rule-bound traditions are admittedly more oral than written.

The best stimulus, therefore, to a people in favor of innovativeness and entrepreneurship is the gospel of Jesus, presented and interpreted in local idiom to ensure that truly progress comes to be from known (customary law) to unknown (the gospel of Jesus).

"FREE TIME"

The question of free time available to Christian leaders is an ongoing one. Some consider the pastor's (or priest's) job to require one-day-per-week and even then he is only "on duty" for a few hours. Yet many pastors do not have other full or part-time employment. Something else must be occupying the rest of this time.

Without getting embroiled in the above discussion, suffice it to say that priests and pastors have in history and contemporary society often been able to pursue issues that others have relatively-speaking had to neglect. Their concerns with people's souls and spiritual well-being prompt them to engage with critical questions regarding the life of the communities they are serving. Christian leaders have been leading innovators and forward thinkers. This has contributed to the church's role in establishing schools and universities—a role that is, according to Mangalwadi, unique to Christianity (as mentioned above[50]). Admittedly as pointed out in chapter 4, liberals have of late been more active in academia than have conservatives, more of whom tend to be Christian.[51] This may or may not be a good thing for academia—academia's losing touch with its roots may bring or be bringing serious issues. As mentioned above, we should also remember that liberalism is itself a product of Christianity.

In my personal experience of living in Africa I can also throw in another suggestion. That is to say, that many people in traditional Africa have what we in the West could call "free time." That free time can be used in endless ways: "just" talking, playing checkers, drinking alcohol, seducing women, sleeping and resting, and so on. Christian leaders who take pastoral care of communities are in my experience the ones most likely to be spending their free time in challenging pursuits that pursue the upbuilding of the whole community. Christian leaders are working on the basis of an authority system that allows them to engage critically with their people's traditions. This perhaps arguably to some but clearly to others, is

50. Mangalwadi, *Book That Made*, 194.
51. As discussed by Greeley and Hout in *Truth About Conservative*, 69.

an avenue through which godliness can lead to the types of self-awareness that can enable strategies that can help to overcome poverty.

Mangalwadi develops a thesis in which he argues that the free time enabled by the discipline of monastic living has been foundational to the legacy of the foundations of modern and "developed" existence. Unlike other monastic traditions,[52] for Christian monks poverty and begging are not foundational values. Unlike monks of other traditions, Christian monks did not despise manual labor.[53]

ALL OF THEOLOGY

I cannot in this chapter exhaust all of Christian theology. It is not without reason that despite the threats to it brought about by so called secularism, modernity, consumerism, and so forth—the church continues to show enormous vitality in the West—in Europe as well as in America. We could say that: God's way is alive and kicking.[54]

Much of that vitality is passed over by contemporary media. Media reporting using European languages is to different degrees rooted in positivist philosophy. Hence in the dualistic West that dominates the media sphere, reporting tends to function at the "real" end of the real versus not-real (or material versus spiritual) dualistic dichotomy. This is striking to me in Africa. In many parts of Africa it is the Christian church, even if divided into numerous sects, that is holding the fabric of society together. The same are being ignored by the media and other official communication channels. Even Geoffrey Sachs' Millennium Project innovations, that are far from overtly Christian seemed, without comment, to use church buildings for almost all of their public meetings in my area of Kenya.[55]

---

52. Here reference is especially to Buddhist monasteries.

53. Mangalwadi, *Book That Made*, 109.

54. While the press these days seems to like to talk-down Christianity and to emphasize ways in which the church is in decline, this should not have us forget the incredibly powerful influence that continues to be there today. For example, this report that talks about a "plunge" in church attendance, at the same time states that 765,000 people attend Anglican churches in the UK every week. That is a phenomenal number of people paying a great deal of attention to something that Dawkins considers to be a delusion (*God Delusion*). http://www.telegraph.co.uk/news/religion/12095251/Church-of-England-attendance-plunges-to-record-low.html.

55. This is a casual observation. I do not have statistics to back this observation.

Perhaps one thing underlying recent opposition in the West to the Christian church is the fact that living a truly Christian life is difficult. Here I agree. I hope my reader will not take this chapter as being a glorious proclamation of the victory of the church in the world. I believe that the victorious one is to be God himself. It is amazing what he has already done using weak and flawed human vessels who become disciples of Jesus. That does not mean that being a Christian who can be used by God is easy.

There is little doubt in my own mind that premier intercultural communication and engagement by the West urgently needs to be placed on an overtly Christian footing. Development intervention, aid provision, medical programs, and numerous other interventionary strategies that attempt to ignore the Bible and the Christian foundation of western culture are asking for trouble. I have given a long list of examples, each one expanded with detailed articulation of how it can or cannot work for western interventions into Africa. The Christian missionary, foibles and all, is the premier role model for intercultural intervention into the majority world. He should be recognized as such by both Christian and so-called secular authorities in the West.

8

International Communication, God, and Evil

I EXPLORED ENDLESS WAYS in chapter 7 in which effective intercultural communication must be rooted in a non-dichotomous ontology. To ignore God's role in intercultural communication is to misunderstand one another. Such misunderstanding can very quickly get very serious.

The length and breadth of the impact of the undermining of the recently-constructed but artificial divide between religion and secular seems to be almost endless. Even if without realizing it, the West has constantly presupposed the above distinction in its international and intercultural relationships. A key presupposition that arises from it is that the secular and the religious can be teased apart. The religious has recently been taken by some as if it is a foreign body parasitizing an otherwise peaceful secular community or person, often bringing violence and dissension.[1] I have shown that this is simply not the case, and the implications for this ontological shift are widespread. Foundation stones naively laid in the twentieth century, with the thought at the time that they would be there forever, now look fundamentally faulty.

Just by way of an example that I will allude to, but that I will not look at in depth, is the globalized educational system. Education has come from Europe to Africa. Modern education in Europe is built on the assumption that such a thing as a "non-religious" foundation exists. Typically, religious studies or something of that ilk, is simply one of a series of courses taught to students, suggesting or presupposing that religion can be singled out and dealt with separately from the rest of life. The same educational system

---

1. Cavanaugh, *Myth of Religious Violence*, 225.

has been transplanted to Africa from the colonial era and on. Anglophone African countries have acquired the British educational system, simply adjusted at the edges, presented in the English language. The theory behind using this educational system in Africa is that it is rooted in a secular objectivity. African people appropriating the education are supposed to be able to separate out their religion(s) from the rest of life, to be left with a pure functional basis of understanding that will help to propel them into the modern world. If, on the other hand, the religious and the secular cannot ever be teased apart, i.e., there is no pure secular, then this educational system may be generating dependency rather than productivity. In fact this seems to be happening. The more educated Africa becomes, the more astute it becomes in drawing resources from Europe or America (i.e., the West) while being able to do relatively little by itself. It could be argued that western education and language has undermined people's independent capabilities and replaced such capabilities with dependence on the West.

I have mentioned above that missionaries have at times chosen to learn from the secular. This especially as they have sought to help to promote development as a means of relieving poverty. Hence some missionaries and Christian initiatives in general from the West in Africa today are prioritizing social action over gospel evangelism. This is labelled as a holistic or integral way of doing mission. (Arthur comments that "integral mission" is increasingly a cover used to justify social action by Christians who seem not to know what to do with the Gospel.[2]) There are various reasons why unfortunately this process often does not bring the anticipated fruit. What can be created is dependency on western people, western thinking and western aid. Samuel and Sugden comment:

> Multinational mission agencies find it very hard to listen to critical questions raised by the Scripture about their activities. They have their own limited agenda, and plead that they must fulfil their supporters' expectations. A recommendation at a recent international conference that relief and development agencies might try to educate First-World supporters about the real situation in the Third World, and its relation to the First World, was greeted by a prediction that 90 percent of the agencies' income would disappear if such programs were introduced.[3]

---

2. http://www.kouya.net/?p=7173.
3. Samuel and Sugden, "Mission Agencies," 154.

International Communication, God, and Evil

As someone who has lived in one African community for over 22 years, I have often endeavored to get Westerners to realize that they do not actually understand what is going on. My attempts tend to fall flat! Africans themselves are not in favor of the idea that Westerners do not understand them, as that has implications for receipt of funds and their own roles in the implementation of projects. Westerners are offended by suggestions that their understanding is too limited for them to engage in projects in Africa. This especially because nationals can be praising them for their activities. They also deeply resent the implication that they need familiarity with local context, culture and language in order to communicate effectively. The implications of this are indeed enormous. Yet try I feel I must to reduce the messes being propagated as a result of the naive foundations on which intervention by the West these days often builds.

I wish there was a way of writing that showed that one has tears in one's eyes and that one is kneeling on the ground. Westerners can take an attack on their capability at penetrating interculturally as an attack on them. Then, when they feel threatened, their response can be to counter-attack. Then they can take the person who seems to be trying to undermine what they are doing as conceited and proud as well as narrow-minded. All the while African nationals may well be backing them up, as the loss of income implied by the withdrawal of foreign-funded projects is a greater calamity than many African people can bear to think about. It is sad when it is people's ego building on translation-failure that stands in the way of doing God's work. It is sad when attempts to increase human flourishing are thwarted by cross-cultural translation failures due to people's egos.

Many interventionary development projects of the type practiced today are beyond effective evaluation. This means that whether or not they are actually "helping" is largely guesswork at best or plain deception at worst. I do not see this situation as needing ever more cleverly honed evaluative tools. I see it as needing to say to some "please stop what you are doing and think again."[4] That is to say "stop" until you can come back with a message about God. I am sorry to be so blunt. I am trying to be honest.

Ignorance in interfering in someone else's business is probably not new. What is relatively new is the widespread use of power without responsibility. Responsibility for a situation requires an ongoing commitment to that in which one is intervening. Ignorance for example in child-rearing is probably normal. Mistakes are no doubt being made constantly by no end

---

4. I hope my reader will note that I am saying this to some and not to all.

of parents. Commitment demonstrating responsibility is however also normal. That is to say: parents do not "experiment" on their children for two weeks and then abandon them. The parent knows that mishandling of the child-rearing process is likely to result in ongoing problems for them for the rest of their lives. So then, a wise dedication to their children can bring good fruit to them for many years to come. This is very different to the widespread contemporary situation of intercultural intervention in which a Westerner flies into an African context, makes friends, makes decisions, invests money, and disappears again. All of course in their own language that has categories, just for example that of "religion" versus "secular," vastly different to the ones an African is typically presupposing.

I would like to emphasize again just how I am saying "stop." I would like to suggest that *some* "stop." Not that they stop, and then disappear off the scene. But that they "stop" one kind of intervention, then engage in another. The "other" which I am advocating is that known as vulnerable mission. That is, intervention based in the use of local languages that is not based on outside resources. For a case study of how this has actually happened amongst some missionaries in Argentina, see Buckwalter and Buckwalter, "Inculturation of the Gospel," 157–60. Mennonite missionary practice in the Argentinian Chaco amongst Toba Qom people provides an excellent case study reflecting many of the practices of "vulnerable mission" that I am advocating. Mennonites started work amongst the Toba-Qom in the 1940s. Realizing the way they were being received, caused them to make a radical change to their missionary style. They have been implementing a "vulnerable" style of ministry from the 1950s to date.[5] They stopped what they were doing. They thought about leaving the field altogether, so discouraging was what they saw. Instead though they decided to stay around, but to work differently.[6]

It can be horrifying to think that perhaps the same faulty logic that sometimes guides mission and development is also being used in other fields. Certainly in secular development practice it seems to be there, and probably one can say even more so than in Christian practice. What then of the level of international diplomacy? What of at the level of counter-terrorism and warfare? Are the likes of President of the USA Barack Obama and the United Nations, for all their extensive networks and capabilities, doing little better at intercultural communication than is the typical missionary?

5. Horst et al., *Mission Without Conquest*.
6. Presentation given by Frank Paul in Kisumu, Kenya on November 19, 2015.

INTERNATIONAL COMMUNICATION, GOD, AND EVIL

Are they making the same kinds of assumptions based on misguided belief in the universality of the category of secularism as being something that is distinct from religion? Is that the basis on which they decide whose side to take in a battle, where to drop the smart-bomb, or who to knock out with a drone? The mind boggles. The very thought that such might be the case is horrifying. Graeme Wood seems to suggest that it is: Major General Michael K. Nagata, the Special Operations commander for the United States in the Middle East, admitting that he had hardly begun figuring out the Islamic State's appeal. "We have not defeated the idea," he said. "We do not even understand the idea."[7]

TRANSLATION DOES NOT WORK

What I am saying in a sense in the above is—that *translation does not work*. Or at least, that it does not work in as reliable a way as is often implicitly conceived or assumed. There are very good reasons for saying that translation (from one language and cultural system to another) does not work. Pragmatically speaking at the same time, translation being the best we have in our current world, seems to be better than nothing. Translation is going on all around us. We may be in a real fix. How on earth do we expect to communicate anything at all in our multicultural world without translation? So then, if translation does not work, what are we going to do about it?

There may be as many answers and response to these questions as there are different scholars. Nevertheless, I want to focus on two responses to it that I believe to be particularly critical. I have already to some extent addressed both of these responses above. I now look at them in more detail.

1. The necessary centrality of the Christian faith in global affairs

    I believe that much of the context of this book points to the necessary centrality of the Christian faith in global affairs. This is both a. as a means of holding together what is extant, and b. a means of helping majority-world people thus contributing to human flourishing in the majority world.

    a. Western secular society these days holds on to the outcomes of Christian belief, while denying their origins. Many secularist practices have emerged from the church. Denying such is like talking about the functions of somebody's body without

7. Wood, "What ISIS Really Wants."

ever making reference to their head. One can go a long way in describing the dexterity of the hand, the capability of the muscles of the leg, the nature of the reproductive functions, and so on without reference to the brain that is located in the head. Something fundamental will be missing from such discussion of the human body, however. This is the nature of academia in today's world (comparable to Goulet's "one eyed giants" in the development world[8]). It is much about form,[9] but as a result of omitting the head (who is Christ) little about purpose, destiny, meaning, value, and eternity. It is the Christian church that roots the West's meanings. Ignoring it is talk without foundation.

b. The means I refer to of empowering the majority world are diverse. It is fundamentally a means which says: give God charge. More specifically (but still quite generally), the church has many recognized roles in a human community. Many we have already touched upon. Let me mention one of which we have not yet made much mention: the church brings unity. Churches are inter-ethnic. Hence they were the first true multinational.[10] Some churches may be very mono-ethnic. While it is not wrong for a church to be so, the claims of the gospel are at the same time quite clearly universal. Jesus did not come to save only one Chinese tribe or a European ethnic enclave. Therefore, the church carries a certain unique dynamic tension. It is perfectly capable of functioning intra-ethnically, while also being oriented to inter-ethnicity.

A local church can be very influential over the lives of many people in the community it serves. It can, and often does, penetrate into almost every nook and cranny of life. When it does this it acquires a unique authority. While "a very powerful organization" (as above) it is simultaneously very weak. The combination of its strength and its weakness enables it to function in a dualistic way. The church can remain distinct from politically powerful institutions. That is: the church influences the powerful, but does

---

8. Goulet, "Development Experts."

9. Fauconnier and Turner refer to this as "form," and tell us that "form is not substance" (*Way We Think*, 4).

10. "Some argue that the Knights Templar (founded in 1118) [a Catholic order] became a multinational in 1135." http://vle.du.ac.in/mod/book/print.php?id=8547&chapterid=11338.

not need them in order to stand, and does not collapse when they fall. Instead, empires come and go, but the church continues through them all, flexing and changing shape with the context of the time.

The above may not be true for every case, but, as a general trend I believe is very much the case. Denying the majority world the church is frankly a cruel outcome of a harsh judgement. I think one can go further and say—that it is cruel to do anything short of using every available means to encourage the church in the majority world, Africa being our case in point.[11] The church emboldens, develops, flexes, empowers, regulates, inspires, encourages, and enables in endless ways. Mignolo shares the following:

> Once upon a time scholars assumed that the knowing subject in the disciplines is transparent, disincorporated from the known and untouched by the geo-political configuration of the world in which people are racially ranked and regions are racially configured. From a detached and neutral point of observation . . . the knowing subject maps the world and its problems, classifies people and projects into what is good for them. Today that assumption is no longer tenable, although there are still many believers.[12]

The "base" on which understanding could be built was until recently thought to lie in objectivity, science, and rationality. Generations of European people have believed themselves as a result to be connected to ultimate truth. Post-modernism has demonstrated that notions of the existence of objectivity and science are contingent and not foundational.[13] They cannot, as a result, provide a genuine foundation for a globalized intercultural unity. The church can provide such a necessary epistemological "base" from which society of the nature which the West values can operate. This was already the role of the church, until for some recently modernism has become hegemonic.

---

11. Just how to encourage the church is another question, also considered in various parts of this text. Testimonies of faith could be said to be a bedrock of Christianity. The currency of the church is, I suggest, faith, and not money.

12. Mignolo, "Epistemic Disobedience," 2.

13. Plantinga, "Reason and Belief," 62.

2. The need for translation to be from unknown to known

This is a very different point, although it also has something in common with the first on the church above. Number 1 above is concerned with giving translation, interpretation and communication a base to work from. My second point here emphasizes the need for translation to be from unknown to known. There may be a place for translation from known to unknown. But in our contemporary world I suggest that translation from unknown to known is desperately missing. *My reader should appreciate that to translate from unknown to known is for receivers of translation to learn from known to unknown.* It is widely appreciated that education should go from known to unknown. For education to go from known to unknown, inputs to education should be "known." Inputs to education are not "known" if they are provided by outsiders to the community being educated. (My reader will note that I have already touched on this issue earlier in this book. I consider it again here because it is very central to my main thrust.)

What do I mean by the above? Simply speaking, I am responding to the fact that increasingly and almost universally, translation from outside of the West into the West is done by non-Westerners. Africa is our focus in this book. There are millions of Africans who almost daily engage in implicit or explicit translation from their own languages and traditions into English. That is to say that they are, whether they know it or not, as far as the West is concerned,[14] translating into what is foreign (i.e., unknown). I would not be surprised if there were less than 50 people in the whole continent translating for the benefit of the West from the unknown, i.e., Westerners translating Africa (their "unknown") for the West (their known). Let us take journalists for example. How many western journalists writing about Africa in English (or other European languages) for the West are writing from the foundation of themselves having a profound understanding of an African language and culture? Perhaps zero. Instead, journalists acquire what they subsequently share from African people who translate into English for them. To do such, I suggest, is a very serious lapse.[15]

14. If we take the example of English, African people may take English as being one of "their" languages, i.e., English as being an African language. Unfortunately that does not stop Westerners from understanding English in profoundly different ways than do Africans.

15. To my understanding here, translating from unknown to known means learning

Scholars are unfortunately little different. Even anthropologists, renowned for the efforts they are making at understanding the "other," these days increasingly rely on local informants to give them insights in European languages. It is rare to find anthropologists designing their theses on the basis of an already existing profound knowledge of the culture and language of the people they are exploring. Almost universally, people doing anthropological research learn from other Westerners who have been informed by non-Westerners using western languages, and from their own informants who also "inform them" using English. I take Gifford here as my example of a scholar who does this.[16] Gifford engages with Kenya's serious daily newspapers, which are according to him "frequently perceptive, enlightening and suggestive for further research ... in much of this book it is their questions I am addressing, their debates I am joining—often their observations and data that I am building on"[17] so that "my focus is ... predominantly English speaking."[18] Gifford, Emeritus Professor of SOAS (School of Oriental and African Studies, London), is writing and publishing books while apparently drawing almost entirely on African educated classes' writing in the colonial language.

It is normal, I suggest, to learn about what is foreign by acquiring something from the unknown to bring into the known. This process results in the building up of a body of knowledge about what is foreign. At the same time it is important to realize that an indigenous understanding of what is being observed by those "foreign" people may be very different from understanding acquired of them as "foreigners." Let us take for example the practice of polygyny in Africa. Westerners, in my experience, almost always look at polygyny negatively. Indigenous people who practice polygyny on the other hand often value it.[19] Whether polygyny is good or bad therefore depends on who is doing the interpreting. An African interpreting into the West may simply presuppose it to be good. A Westerner interpreting

---

from people's use of their first languages and not from their uses of global languages such as English.

16. Gifford, *Christianity, Politics*.
17. Ibid., 2.
18. Ibid., 4.
19. Prohibitions against polygyny tend to lose out when legal systems are transferred from the West to Africa. Gillespie and Nicholson, *Law and Development*, 299.

into the West who wants western people to know that it is good would be required to first make a case for such. In other words, the African's evaluation of "good" is, as far as the West is concerned, wrong. That evaluation conceals a difference which in this case is an "evil" from a western perspective. The more the African person's translation remains dominant, the more that "evils" (in this case, or more generally "unknowns") will be concealed. Translation of this nature from an African's known into an unknown (to him) western culture, will conceal more and more. It can take us to a point at which pretty much all difference will be rendered out of sight.

Allow me to give another example. Let us imagine that the grass is blue in Africa but green in Europe. An African coming to Europe will say "our grass is blue." The Europeans will say "oh, then what you call blue is what we call green." The African will go back and tell his people that in the European language blue is green. All may seem to be well, i.e., this anomaly or difference may not be discovered, until one day a Westerner actually goes to Africa to look at the grass. A Westerner going to Africa will immediately be shocked to find grass to be of a different color. Going back to the West the Westerner will say "the grass that African people say is green is actually blue!" It should be evident that to make this revelation Westerners will need to take the trouble to explore Africa as it is. They cannot rely on the Africans' words. Because this is these days happening less and less, i.e., as mentioned above more and more translation into western languages is being done by non-Westerners, more and more African truths are staying out of sight to the West. Sometimes the problem here is that even should a Westerner proclaim that "in Africa the grass is blue," other Westerners may choose not to believe this, as they have decided that they should learn about Africa from the African and not from the Westerner. Often fear of being accused of racism underlies such orientations to preferred patterns of learning, that is, it would be "racist" to assume that a Westerner can teach another Westerner about African culture more accurately than an African can. If or when Westerners are ready to listen to their western colleague who has knowledge of an African language as used in context, then they will have been enabled to learn of otherwise occluded but extant differences. The extent of these differences might be colossal.

International Communication, God, and Evil

Relying on foreigners for one's information about a foreign country and people is always problematic. Two epistemologies will clash; that of how a foreigner uses English to describe what they see, and that which a native English speaker would say in English after observing the foreign. When, as in today's world, the former is given preference, cultural gaps and differences are very effectively concealed.

I could ask: who is the best person to teach Kenyan people (I have lived in Kenya since 1993) about England? Frankly, when a Kenyan talks about England, he or she will talk about it in a way that Kenyans will understand. This may be very different indeed to the way that I, as someone born and raised in Britain in a white family, might understand it. I suggest that the Kenyan who has spent some time in England is in many ways much better equipped to explain Britain to Kenyan people than I am. He notes things that Kenyans would note in the way Kenyans would note them. I, on the other hand, understand England as a native-born Englishman. It is very hard, actually it is impossible, for me to grasp how a Kenyan person might understand England.[20]

The above raises a set of very profound and serious questions. The principle I espouse above is very rarely taken seriously. The opposite is pretty much always the case. Africans are often busy learning about the West from Westerners. Westerners provide the foundation for what they are to know about the West. One only has to look at the books in African libraries (typically written by Westerners) and the language used in African education. Those books written by African authors are of necessity modelled on western traditions and styles. If for no other reason this is often because funding for publication may only be available to those whose writing pleases Westerners. This means that formal education can never be integrated into people's innate life understanding. It constitutes translation from known (to the Westerner) to unknown (that is, Africa—the Westerner's unknown). As a result, for African people it is always foreign,

---

20. I think it is likely that if a Kenyan were to describe England within earshot that I would instinctively want to correct them. Such an instinct would be based on error. I would be particularly wanting to correct them if they were using English to describe England to their Kenyan colleagues. Their use of English in this way to me constitutes an error. They "should" describe their experience in England to fellow Kenyans using Kenyan language(s). If I become sufficiently familiar with that Kenyan language I may as a result better appreciate what the Kenyan person is trying to say about England. That would require a very close and profound appreciation of the Kenyan language concerned.

distinct, the result of an unknown epistemology. As a result of this practice, the West gets flattened out to appear like Africa (as I have mentioned in reverse above).

In Christian mission circles the view of the foreign missionary in Africa may be considered to be subject to correction by an indigenous person's report on the activity of that missionary, presented in a European language to the West. According to our above analyses, such evaluation is erroneous. This explains why there has over the years been a massive, largely misguided, condemnation of what western missionaries have done in Africa.

A vital corrective to the above is needed at both ends of the Euro/African divide. In Africa, use of indigenous languages by indigenous people should displace the role currently filled by English and western languages and scholars. The West, in order to acquire knowledge of Africa, needs to listen more to western-born people who have acquired experience in Africa, than to Africans born and raised in Africa. That Westerner needs to have learned about Africa through African languages learned from within the culture. The African who wants to tell his people about the West needs to have learned about the West through western languages learned from within the culture. Then let each translate as best they can.

BLIND COMPASSION

Compassion, in many ways, is a great thing but should compassion be blind? Presumably it is better for it not to be "blind." The being "blind" I am referring to here is related to the section above. That is—the fact that many compassionate acts originating from the West are implemented on foundations that have a dubious epistemology from the majority world's perspectives. This is not without its effect. It causes constant tensions and failures.

Let me unpack the above paragraph a little. Compassionate projects in Africa coming from the West are designed using English.[21] Most likely the designers are aware of a need for cultural adjustment to the contexts of implementation. The means through which they meet with and engage the context of implementation though, is these days almost exclusively through translation into English by nationals. This is the means by which they meet all the issues we have discussed above, and more that space has not allowed

21. I will take English here as representing European languages as a whole.

International Communication, God, and Evil

us to discuss.[22] In other words, the language they meet is of a "flattened" African culture, appearing in many ways, or even "as much as possible" to be the same as Western culture. The process of translation especially when combined with power issues, has domesticated African "culture" to appear western.[23] Fortunately or unfortunately, aspects of the culture that had been rendered invisible by the translation process later come to trip up the project. Such "tripping up" is often known as corruption. It is sometimes misleadingly considered to be a "lack of political will."[24] These analyses of project failure are not based on understanding. In project after project, time after time, again and again, "corruption" is blamed for failures in Africa, large and small.[25]

The above blame-game that holds corruption responsible for endless failures in Africa seems to not quite overtly say something about the African people. It seems to imply by slightly tangential means that African people are particularly evil and selfish. It is ironic that such should be implied, while at the same time means used to counter racism overtly deny the existence of such an ethnically-related tendency to "evil." In so far as any "evil selfishness" of African people is there because they have not yet become Christian, the same is concealed by efforts in the West to deny such racially-related correlations in the name of countering racism. The actuality on the ground is, of course, concealed by translation error as I have mentioned above, by which the West builds up its understanding of Africa on a foundation of reports by Africans themselves using western languages. At the end of the day, one does not seem to know which direction one is facing on this issue!

When my research hit this brick wall in about 2002, I refused simply to accept that one population of people can be so much more grossly selfish and evil than another population.[26] My approach to this issue was to ask

---

22. For example, I have in this book not so far mentioned power issues that can have African nationals by all means please the foreigner so as to perpetuate the flow of money regardless of actual "truth."

23. Venuti, *Scandals of Translation*, 5.

24. For discussion of "lack of political will" see: http://www.u4.no/publications/unpacking-the-concept-of-political-will-to-confront-corruption/.

25. See references to Gupta's work on corruption above. A corruption discourse seems to define relationships between many majority world communities and their governments. Perhaps also between these communities and many of the foreign actors who engage them.

26. I accept, and frequently observe, ways in which the West's Christian history has

whether apparent "evil" in Africa might appear so because of foundational cultural differences not usually grasped by the West. Hence I designed my research to be rooted in my comprehension of indigenous languages and through participant observation without any recourse to surveys, questionnaires, or formal interviews.[27] As already mentioned above,[28] apparent "evil," for example a woman's seeming to neglect children she is looking after, can often be understood through attention to African people's understanding of their gods.

Instead of trying to resolve this issue the West tends to push it under the carpet by prohibiting racism. Even when prohibited, racism does not seem to end. The situation of Blacks in the West is not identical to that of those who remain in Africa, but there are definitely parallels. They are also forced to use English to try to articulate themselves to mother-tongue users of the same.[29] The fact that racism takes so much effort to tackle[30] shows how prevalent it actually is in people's minds. I suggest that just bludgeoning people who respond to apparent differences between Blacks and Whites is an insufficient strategy to bring real resolution to the extant issues.

Interestingly, some Blacks in America do seem to have realized that language underlies many of their cultural issues. I have been flummoxed when searching for interest in Swahili on the internet. I am a Swahili speaker and use Swahili on a regular daily basis. Yet, when I search for Swahili on the internet very often I do not find references from East Africa (the home of Swahili), but from Blacks in North America.[31] While their

---

given them a peculiar morality. I contend however that widespread accusations re. levels of immorality in Africa tend to arise from misunderstandings, including from a failure to take into account the impact of the above western Christian history.

27. Harries, "Pragmatic Theory," 31.

28. See chapter 2.

29. I am aware of discussion as to whether Ebonics (the language of black Americans) should be officially accepted as a distinct form of English. Because it is inevitably heavily rooted in western English it may end up being very difficult indeed to keep the two Englishes apart even if this were done. Added to this difficulty, on the basis of what I have seen happen in Africa, where Westerners tend to "do literacy" much more than do African people, production of written forms of Ebonics may become a responsibility of Westerners, which would introduce a double irony.

30. Major efforts to tackle racism in the USA have not prevented enormous protests against its police force: http://www.cbc.ca/news/world/black-lives-matter-police-killings-2015-1.3383282.

31. For example see: http://kuow.org/post/african-americans-and-native-speakers-keep-swahili-language-alive.

efforts at learning Swahili while living in North America are unfortunately unlikely to enable them to throw off the hegemony of English over their lives, this does show that those Blacks are aware of the source of one of their problems: English. Also to be noted about Blacks in the West is their love for Christianity and for the church. My experience with black churches in London tells me that African people can interpret Christianity in their own cultural ways (even when using English). As a result the church becomes a place at which they can be free to behave like Africans! This helps African people to maintain their identity in the diaspora.

To come back to the question of evil above, I do not believe, as the constant condemnation of corruption in Africa implies, that African people are inherently more evil than are Whites. On the other hand, neither do I accept that generations of being guided by Christianity on the side of Westerners has had no impact. I do accept that there are aspects of western culture that are especially moral because of their particular godly origins. The way forward for Africans, I believe, is neither for their culture to be pushed underground (anti-racist legislation) nor for them constantly to be thumped (assuming that project failures arise from their being evil or corrupt), but by taking very seriously their encounter with the living God in the gospel of Jesus Christ. That is to say: any moral superiority of western communities is likely to have arisen from their Christian history. When the West denies this, they are trying to deny Africa access to important truths that could help them enormously.

I will not pretend to be able to solve North America's racist issues, beyond my comment above. I can continue to say though—that use of European languages in Africa is a serious bane that needs urgent attention. While Blacks in North America are struggling to learn some Swahili, all too many Swahili speakers are insufficiently engaged in attempting to understand themselves, and are over-engaged by running away into English. It should perhaps not surprise us at this stage in this book that many have noted that the main institution continent-wide that succeeds in actually using and promoting the use of African languages is the Christian church. "Emergence of the majority of African languages, as written forms [has] come through the agency and the work of Christian missionary groups" Prah tells us in his introduction to his examination of *The Role of Missionaries in the Development of African Languages*.[32] This edited volume contains example after example of ways in which the Christian church helped

---

32. Prah, "Introduction: Winning Souls," 1.

and helps to maintain African languages and traditions. Sometimes *only* churches maintain this role: "the churches in Cameroon are duly considered the only institutions that effectively ensure the promotion and survival of the local languages."[33] The church more than any other institution helps the African to be himself.

WE SHOULD SHARE GOD

I had in my younger years much the same issue that I perceive continues to trouble western people about God. It is the same issue that gives Dawkins his following and his fame. This issue has confused development experts into thinking that English will work for Africa, because what is under consideration is what is "real." It is the conundrum faced by dualistic people of trying to get God to fit into the category that they call "real." Dawkins tells us that he does not fit, as a result of which he concludes that he does not "exist." I do not think that is a very satisfactory solution for today's world. The problem is actually not with God, but with the category into which we are trying to squeeze him. If the category is wrong, then it is no wonder that God might not be ready to be confined by it.

That is not the only objection I had to faith in God during my youth. An allegiance to God can also feel like a losing of control. As a lad brought up in "secular" UK, I wanted to exhibit (supposed) strengths that faith in God seemed to deny me. Now I can see that those strengths were a bit of a deception. There might just be a few strong men out there who can, like Hollywood heroes, by sheer rational conviction and gritted determination overcome one obstacle after another in their lives, for a period.[34] Recent reports from America about my generation of white males that talk about a spike in suicides and deaths related to drug addiction, however, also seem to show that it does not always work.[35]

Becoming a Christian involves some compromises to one's ego. It involves "followership," at times, as well as leadership at others. It involves

33. Bitjaa-Kody and Ndjonmbog, "Involvement of Churches," 229.

34. John Wayne comes to mind (http://www.imdb.com/name/nm0000078/bio?ref_=nm_ov_bio_sm). I have never been a great TV watcher, but I guess stars like John Wayne did have an impact on my young mind. Much of that impact might have been positive. At the same time, I look back on Hollywood heroism as a bit of a deception.

35. http://www.iflscience.com/health-and-medicine/rising-death-rates-among-middle-aged-white-americans-due-epidemic-drugs-alcohol.

concessions to a greater power than oneself. Being a Christian can be difficult. Prayer, I still find difficult. I suspect I am not alone in that. I want to pray more, but this world comes to be just too absorbing (things that Luhrmann very articulately points out for western Christians).[36] In that sense, what in my mind I might have been (that strong rational male of the movies and ideals) limps a little. I guess he has met one who is stronger than himself. I have had to conclude—that actually it was my faith in that strong rational western male that was misguided. Not my faith in Christ. It is faith in Christ that works.

Sharing God with other people starts when one dies to oneself. From there on you do what you can. Actually it comes to be not you doing it in your own strength, but God in you. I can't articulate all the rest of what it means to be a Christian believer here. Many books have been written on that topic. Many more continue to be written. I encourage my reader to explore.

Is God real or not, was the wrong question. Is God essential? Yes. For this to be known is important, if not vital, for development in Africa, and for justice as we know it.

---

36. Luhrmann points to the difficulty of having faith in God and believing that he is listening to us (*When God Talks*, xxii).

Summary

THE READER SHOULD NOTE that because this is a summary it does not fully articulate or substantiate all the claims that it makes. Substantiation will be found in the chapters concerned. The summary is best read after reading the main text, as a reminder of some of the most important points made in the book.

Chapter 1 points to recent literature that has demonstrated a high degree of illegitimacy of the apparently common sense category of "religion" in English. This chapter suggests, through reference to the literature, that what is commonly in English called "religion" is actually that which resembles western Protestant Christianity. As a result use of the label religion for that which is not western Protestantism can be to misleadingly domesticate it into non-native skin. I suggest that the implications of this shift in the understanding of the concept "religion" are vast. This book only begins to examine these implications.

I suggest in this chapter that for non-Westerners the "religious" is indistinguishable from the "secular" part of their lives. By way of example, I suggest that witchcraft beliefs, which are often considered to be widespread in Africa, cannot be excised and discarded in favor of modernism. So then witchcraft beliefs are not just a product of a lack of "developed awareness" that Horton suggested.[1] Evans-Pritchard suggests that a Zande (the Sudanese people on which he carried out his classic study of witchcraft) person "cannot get out of [the] meshes [of his witchcraft beliefs] because it is the only world he knows . . . [and] is the texture of his thought and he cannot

1. Horton, *Patterns of Thought*, 222.

think that his thought is wrong."[2] I suggest that "witchcraft beliefs" are an integral part of who African people are and need, in order to contribute to human flourishing, to be transformed, not enlightened.

I argue that taking "religion" out of the equation results in fundamental transformation of the relationship between scholarly disciplines as applied to Africa. This implies the need for major revisions throughout western academia. I suggest in *chapter 1* that English itself is implicated in this need for major revision. Because it is implicitly dualistic, contemporary English presupposes the religion versus secular divide. As a result, holistic African uses of English clash with dualistic western ones. Not to use English dualistically, i.e., on the basis of separation of the "religious" and the "secular," is to abuse it. It seems then that for English to be used to blaze a different trail will of necessity require *abuses* of English.

Why do 100% of African people seem to believe in God whereas many Westerners do not? *Chapter 2* suggests that this is, in part at least, due to some logical errors made by the West, whereby not believing "something about" God is interpreted as not believing in him at all. For Africans, for whom God is often implicitly understood as being "the helpful one" who solves their problems, it makes no sense to reject "belief in" him. Contrary to widespread understanding, I suggest in this chapter that African belief in God does not rubber stamp what "religious" Westerners call the "supernatural." For many African people, who I argue have no belief in the natural for something to be super of, that something should be supernatural is inconceivable. Muddling belief in the supernatural with faith in God seems to have brought much confusion to the West. In short I suggest in *chapter 2* that Westerners may reject belief in God on the basis that he is not in a category, which category itself makes no sense to Africans in the first place.

In my youth, I found the basis on which people were rejecting faith in God to be dubious. I refused to share in what I saw as a narrow "rejection," preferring to follow the wisdom of older people. In due course I found that people who rejected Christianity built their rejection on the back of beliefs that historically arose from Christianity. One question asked in *chapter 2* is: what does it mean to "reject" something while building on the foundations laid by that which you are rejecting?

As a young Christian, convinced that I should use my life in loving service to God, long-term service amongst the poor seemed the way to go. I now seek to educate the West about what I have learned to date in following

2. Evans-Pritchard, *Witchcraft, Oracles*, 95.

that call. I believe that it is sometimes more important to be honest than just to say what Westerners want to hear. Orienting western people who come to Africa can be difficult, especially if their horizon is short-term. Short-termers can in Africa end up valued primarily for their money. To get beyond such valuation requires, I suggest in *chapter* 2, long-term commitment from the start, plus use of local languages and local resources.

Chapter 2 further suggests that if we could get away from contemporary positivistic historical analysis engaged by historians, the media, and others, we would find the impact of the Christian faith on the West to have been enormous and transformative. Perception of the same transformative power has Africans flock to churches today. Grasping the nature of "witchcraft" and "fear of ancestors" I suggest is key to understanding African ways of life, that from a European vantage point have a lot in common around the continent.

Traditions that respond to witches and ancestors are not, according to arguments presented below, a fog that will magically lift away from the African continent. Rather, fear of witches and respect for ancestors define people's very being. Transforming these kinds of thinking is an involved task requiring godly input. I suggest that African tradition is more likely to bow to revelations about God than it is to articulations of "nature" or "reason."

Christians in Africa may be continuing to presuppose the need for adherence to traditional laws. Traditional laws uphold people's life-absorbing traditions and are at times, as demonstrated in this chapter, ignored on pain of death. I argue that African people often do not question the enormous damage perceived to be done by envy, even if the envious person (i.e., the witch) is unaware of the impact that their thoughts are having. Witchcraft in Africa I suggest is "ordinary." It can be used to deter various unsociable behaviors. The fact that "spiritual" Christian practice can sometimes undermine these deterrents can make people reluctant to join certain churches. In *chapter* 2 I argue that justice tends in Africa to be extra-rational, including instant justice meted out because formal courts (a legal system introduced from the West) are unreliable. This is in some ways akin to Old Testament justice.

Because of the above, God (god) is in Africa a daily reality. To say God is a delusion seems to be a strange western mannerism. This is not to claim that African people will necessarily agree with all that I write in this vein. Translation to the West from Africa is a complex contested arena. I write

Summary

as a Westerner who has had exposure to Africa. This puts me in a different position to Africans who have had exposure to the West. Even if I do not really "get" Africa, we should remember, I suggest, as well though that neither do Africans who use English necessarily "get" the West.

Evolutionary advantage may not coincide with accurate perceptions of reality, suggests Hoffman, whose presentation forms the basis for the discussion in *chapter 3*. If "reality" (i.e., nature, objectivity) perceived by Europeans is not universal, then this implies that modern man may have lost the foundation of communication with cultural others in which he has been believing. If "the real" is not common between Europe and Africa, then a question I ask in this chapter is: what common basis is there for intercultural communication? Africa borrows enormously from Europe. It often seems to be under bombardment with things from the West. Africa uses the resultant borrowed front to communicate back what Europeans like to see and hear. Following some of the above, I suggest that perhaps Europeans' understanding of African people and societies is more limited than they like to think.

Being honest about African reality puts me at risk of accusations of racism by Europeans. I suggest in *chapter 3* that what is honesty to Europeans may appear dishonest to some Africans' self-understanding and perception of the meaning of English words. For example, I might suggest that we do not have "love" in Africa as love is understood in Europe. This is because European notions of love are rooted in centuries of Christian influence that Africa has not shared. To "believe" and to "agree," two different things in Europe, can be indistinguishable for some African people. Material and spiritual in much of Africa are not distinct, I suggest. Ancestors sometimes form the closest equivalent to western notions of what is "real" through their linking behavior with consequences. Ironically, the very God some in Europe recently think to be *delusion*,[3] I propose to be a potential common foundation who can enable comprehension across cultural chasms.

What foundation do scholars work on, is a question asked in *chapter 4*. The notion that discussion between scholars will reveal truth is in this chapter identified as being a peculiar one and a Christian one. The soft underbelly of liberalism, an essentially modern and secular approach to life popular in the West today, is its faith in the existence and comprehensibility of truth. (I appreciate that it is very difficult to define "liberalism." I largely

---

3. I here make implicit reference to Richard Dawkins' book entitled *The God Delusion*.

Summary

take Siedentop's view of the history of the term.[4] Liberalism, I suggest, believes that truth is to be had, and that it is rooted in nature. Hence liberals, as secularists in general, presuppose a religious versus secular divide and for their own purposes "believe in" the latter, i.e., in nature. The ability to presuppose such a distinction, I argue in this chapter, requires imagination. I take imagination as being a normal and necessary part of human thinking and understanding. Classifying people's imaginings about the divine on the side of "nature" is such a stretch that it in the end, I suggest, delegitimizes liberalism's supposed epistemological certainty. Imagination challenges nature. Imagination by humans cannot be clearly distinguished from divine intervention. If liberalism acknowledges a role for imagination and the latter cannot be distinguished from divine intervention, then faith in God has become necessary foundation and complement to liberalism.

Chapter 4 argues that liberalism left to its own devices has encouraged slavery for many while seeking freedom for a few. It points out that academia tends to exclude conservative thinkers from its ranks, sometimes actively and sometimes by encouraging their self-elimination. A result of this is that much of academia, especially the globally-dominant United States academic community, may not accurately represent the understanding of its population. In this chapter I ask whether such failure to accurately represent its people might undermine academia's claims to impartiality. Is such bias unacknowledged or even aggressively denied? If so, I suggest in this chapter, this puts the work of liberal/progressive academics up to question.

I suggest that it is the Christian population that has often been the means that has both actualized benefits of liberalism, and mitigated its extremes. Left to its own devices, without a Christian counter, liberalism would be less tolerant and diverse. I share arguments which claim that strategies to counter AIDS in Africa that are based on liberal designs have resulted in millions of preventable deaths. Liberals can react harshly against Christians. I question the legitimacy of such reaction. Liberals who claim to be the fount of the development needed by Africa unfortunately, I suggest in this chapter, all too often set a trajectory of ongoing dependency on what appear to the non-West to be mystical erudite sources of knowledge. Liberals should be open. Thus a helpful road for Africa could include faith in God.

Chapter 5 concentrates on anthropologist Luhrmann's explorations of Christian belief in the USA, Asia and Africa. As a secular anthropologist I suggest in *chapter* 5 that Luhrmann is theoretically bound by a dualistic

4. Siedentop, *Inventing the Individual*.

Summary

approach whereby anything that is not "real" does not exist. Hence the need for sub-rational foundations for secular living is obscured from her view. In the same way that Luhrmann's and mainstream anthropologists' theses sink or swim on the back of dualism, I suggest that western Christians at times impose their English categories on theology by insisting that God is "real" and implicitly that African Christianity needs westernizing. Christian believers should be challenged but not threatened by academia's strong attachment to strict dualism, which may be exposing anthropology's vulnerability to theology. In fact, Luhrmann's perception of the church as "good" seems to tie in with African notions that God should be valued for what he does.

In this chapter I suggest that non-western holistic contexts that operate using different categories seem to problematize the Western dualistic stance. This raises the question of whether Luhrmann's pronouncements might sometimes undermine pastoral approaches at countering "evil" that, in her determination to stick to "reality" only, she appears to miss. Seen from holistic perspective dualistic ideas that God must not be "in one's head," that God equals "supernatural," that one can understand English language interpretations of events from around the world, that "religion" is a legitimate category, that imagination is distinct from divine intervention, should according to arguments presented in *chapter* 5, raise questions about the applicability of some of Luhrmann's intercultural research outcomes. I argue that western assumptions that can render God a delusion do not transfer interculturally. Might Luhrmann's "theories of mind" be little different from a re-invention of the need for theology to underlie intercultural engagement, by a different name? I argue that academia's preconceived dualistic perspective throws, for those who have the eyes to see them, fascinating shadows on the contexts Luhrmann explores. Academia's presupposition of God's unreality reveals, according to my analysis in *chapter* 5, fault lines in western thinking.

Everybody wants to prosper, Westerner and African alike, we learn in *chapter* 6. Focus on the "real" in the West has apparently marginalized God's role in people's acquisition of prosperity. Yet at the same time I point out that a high percentage of people in the West consider themselves to be Christian. Neither western nor any other thinking can be theologically "neutral," and so I argue in this chapter that theology these days spreads incognito. Human rights, considered to be a non-religious subject have, according to an argument presented in this chapter, actually grown out of Christian theology. This chapter suggests that fear of Islam underlies a lot of

Summary

taboos on truth that still trouble the West. Fear of Islam followed by identification of Islam as a "religion" akin to Christianity has, I suggest, resulted in many illegitimate efforts at drawing parallels between the two. This chapter asks whether this has contributed to recent efforts at re-interpreting history and condemning the use of Scriptures in public debate. While African people generally don't swallow the above (it only really makes sense in the light of a dualistic context) they are obliged, I argue in this chapter, because of the dominance of the West, to give abeyance. In the light of much of the above and given the implicit relationship between Christianity and development, the West's rejection of Christ has unfortunately effectively been a kicking away of the ladder of development.

Vulnerable strategies that enable close understanding between people from different parts of the world can, I suggest, bring a singular traction to intercultural engagement. I suggest that such traction is unmatched by other development approaches that hit some of the problems alluded to above. Christ, God incarnate, is best shared from a position of vulnerability, this chapter suggests. This chapter further argues that those who follow the West for its power might unexpectedly find that the West's faith (or lack of faith) can disallow means of communication and engagement that mutual faith in God ought to facilitate. Contrary to the West, Africa aspires to wealth by spiritual means.[5] Given the West's history of determined secularism, I argue that those means prove hard for Westerners to grasp. Roles for God in Africa seem in the English language to fall under the western category of "chance." When Westerners hear an African speak in English about roles for God, they may be falsely assuming that Africans are operating from the same category of "chance" as they are. Western English, it is suggested in *chapter 6*, has itself been shorn of its one-time holistic content.

The integral relationship in Africa between "God" and searches for fortune (and protection from powers that counter fortune) is, it is suggested in *chapter 6*, much stronger than many Westerners seem to realize. The desire for fortune, it could be said, is the reason for many Africans to believe in and follow that which English translates "god." But yet, Westerners also desire fortune. This chapter suggests that sub-rational beliefs often supplement Westerners' search for such. Were they Africans, they may well have those sub-rational beliefs labelled as "god." As a result I argue in this

---

5. The term "spiritual means" is of course necessarily inaccurate as far as Africa is concerned because of the absence of a distinction between the spiritual and the material. I use the term here as a prompt designed to stimulate certain avenues of western thinking.

Summary

chapter that people who in the West are considered to be "atheists," may well be considered, in the light of African categorizations, to believe in God. This means that the apparent choice to not believe might arise in the West from an over narrow definition of god.

In *chapter 7* I suggest that having a history of secularism results in some Westerners preferring to engage interculturally with Africans other than on the back of faith in God. This has resulted in development being seen by some as other than Christianization. At the same time, close examination of the practices of many global bodies would reveal that the Bible remains the unacknowledged source of principles for intercultural engagement and development. So this chapter suggests that while to openly build on biblical foundations is frowned upon, in the international community one has little choice but implicitly to build on the same.

The Bible enables and promotes, when properly understood, (I in this chapter suggest) a profound and essential vulnerability in intercultural relationship. This chapter points to evidence which suggests that missionaries whose message is holistic and who give God's word a high profile can end up greatly valued and trusted by the majority-world communities they serve. On the contrary, the lack of a clear moral stand among some development workers and anthropologists can cause endless difficulties.

The enormous relevance of missionary intervention is, it is suggested in *chapter 7*, related to ways in which cultural traits and behavior are critical to people's state of socio-economic development. Jesus' own teachings strongly opposed the use of money as the primary means to transform lives. Presumably he perceived that such could result in corruption and dependency. Jesus came out instead in favor of holistic (that is theological) challenges. I suggest in *chapter 7* that a missionary's use of indigenous languages and resources can result in the missionary being highly attuned to local contexts. This can in turn bring about ways of working that can be imitated locally. Otherwise issues of understanding, sometimes arising from as simple a tendency as indigenous people's reluctance to say "no" regardless of their own heartfelt lack of appreciation of an issue or question, can complicate what ought to have been simple intervention. These kinds of complications, which often have financial aspects, may end up causing resentment among members of the indigenous communities they are meant to serve. I suggest that because Christian prayer is rarely resented, prayer ministry has much to offer.

It is because people inevitably build their insights on prior understanding that I suggest that a leader in an African church will set out with understanding that arises from African tradition. That tradition includes practices such as so-called witchcraft. Tradition is the starting block. I argue that innovation and entrepreneurship can grow very effectively from deeply-rooted Christian belief that builds on such a starting block. It is the gospel, after all, that has kick started and perpetuated an educated approach to life around the world, I suggest, drawing particularly on Mangalwadi.[6] God's servants whose practices are rooted in the word of God, who are alert to culture, and who have time to seek deep and lasting solutions to people's problems, have the potential to bring beneficial sustainable innovations. This is both thrilling and challenging. The premier intercultural worker, I suggest, is the Christian missionary. I argue in *chapter 7* that only the latter (amongst Westerners) is at least theoretically free from positivistic hang-ups. This is because it is the missionary who has an alternative foundation to positivism from which to engage interculturally. My analysis attempts to show that God's way is alive and kicking, despite opposition from enormous global players (like the media) who root themselves in positivistic philosophies.

The final chapter to this book, *chapter 8*, posits that to ignore God's role in intercultural communication is to generate misunderstanding. Undermining of the presupposed division between the religious and the secular is in *chapter 8* found to have massive implications, including the need to seriously re-evaluate the advisability of the globalization of English language educational systems. Christians have in recent decades come up with integral mission. Unfortunately, I argue in this chapter, the way it is often implemented, this approach risks throwing baby out with the bath water. I argue that there is a need for humility on the side of the West, and a readiness to say "we were wrong." Intervention beyond western shores requires thinking in context; a case study of Mennonites in the Argentine Chaco is given to illustrate how this can work in practice. I go on to argue that issues regarding the limitations of translation go far beyond missionary and development practices and encompass global-level engagements, including the political and military. In this chapter I make the case to say that revision of methods of translating concepts across cultures is badly needed.

Since it is the source of so much western thinking, I suggest in *chapter 8* that Christianity should be at the fulcrum of global affairs. Christ's church, representing his Kingdom on earth, bringing hope and a true epistemological foundation from "weakness," that touches hearts, needs to be encouraged. Understanding the value of implementing an approach to

---

6. Mangalwadi, *Book That Made*.

encouraging of the church in diverse contexts requires, I suggest, translation from unknown to known. That is, a member of a learning community needs to translate for the benefit of their own community, from a position of exposure to the context of the "other." In other words, I argue that someone who is learning about the "other" should not rely on the "other" to explain their meaning to them. This implies a need for Westerners to learn about the world from fellow Westerners who have crossed cultural barriers, and not only from non-Westerners who have acquired English. Similarly, I suggest that for Africans learning about "the other" would be more accurate and helpful if African languages were used as the medium of instruction. If implemented, then this kind of translating, which I suggest is vitally needed, has the potential to expose previously concealed but critical differences between peoples and cultures.

Sometimes western intervention beyond its shores has been motivated by compassion. I argue that it is a perception of corruption, and some kind of presupposition to the effect that non-Westerners are "evil," that has all too often perpetuated a position based on compassion as a justification for ongoing intervention in the majority world. I argue that it would be more appropriate to take a stance that uses vernacular languages, while recognizing the role of the church. One way in which the gospel can make a difference for African people is by allowing the African to be himself. As a result, the primary message of importance that the West has to share is that of their faith in God. That is not the "real" god of dualistic philosophies, or even the god of Hollywood heroism, but the God who is greater than that, and asks his servants to give their lives in his loving service. I suggest that this re-emphasis is most likely to lead to sustainable African development.

Bibliography

Appleby, R. Scott. "Rethinking Fundamentalism in a Secular Age." In *Rethinking Secularism*, edited by Craig Calhoun et al., 225–47. Oxford: Oxford University Press, 2011.
Asad, Talal. "The Construction of Religion as an Anthropological Category." In *A Reader in the Anthropology of Religion*, edited by Michael Lambek, 115–32. Oxford: Blackwell, 2002.
———. *Formations of the Secular: Christianity, Islam, Modernity*. Stanford, CA: Stanford University Press, 1993.
———. "Freedom of Speech and Religious Limitations." In *Rethinking Secularism*, edited by Craig Calhoun et al., 282–97. Oxford: Oxford University Press, 2011.
———. "Reading a Modern Classic: W. C. Smith's *The Meaning and End of Religion*." *History of Religions* 40, no.3 (2001) 205–22.
Bashkow, Ira. *The Meaning of Whitemen: Race and Modernity in the Orokaiva Cultural World*. London: University of Chicago Press, 2006.
Bell, Duncan. "What is Liberalism?" *Political Theory* 42, no.6 (2014) 682–715.
Bendix, Reinhard. *Max Weber: An Intellectual Portrait*. London: University of California Press, 1977.
Berman, Harold Joseph. *Law and Revolution*. Vol. 1, *The Formation of the Western Legal Tradition*. Cambridge, MA: Harvard University Press, 1983.
Bessenecker, Scott A. *Overturning Tables: Freeing Missions From the Christian-Industrial Complex*. Illinois: IVP, 2014.
Bhargava, Rajeev. "Rehabilitating Secularism." In *Rethinking Secularism*, edited by Craig Calhoun et al., 92–113. Oxford: Oxford University Press, 2011.
Bitjaa-Kody, Zachée Denis, and Joseph Roger Ndjonmbog. "The Involvement of Churches in the Development and Promotion of Cameroonian Languages since 1960." In *The Role of Missionaries in the Development of African Languages*, edited by Kwesi Kwaa Prah, 217–30. Cape Town: CASAS, 2009.
Bloch, Maurice. "Why Religion Is Nothing Special But Is Central." *Philosophical Transactions* 363, no.1499 (2008) 2055–61.
Blommaert, Jan, and Jef Verschueren. *Debating Diversity: Analysing the Discourse of Tolerance*. London: Routledge, 1998.

Bibliography

Blunt, Robert. "Satan Is An Imitator: Kenya's Recent Cosmology of Corruption." In *Producing African Futures: Ritual and Reproduction in a Neoliberal Age*, edited by Brad Weiss, 294–328. Leiden: Brill, 2004.

Bronkema, David. "Flying Blind? Christian NGOs and Political Economy." In *Christian Mission and Economic Systems: A Critical Survey of the Cultural and Religious Dimensions of Economies*, edited by John Cheong and Eloise Meneses, 211–45. Pasadena: William Carey Library, 2015.

Buckwalter, Albert, and Lois Buckwalter. "The Inculturation of the Gospel." In *Mission Without Conquest*, Willis Horst et al., 167–72. Carlisle, UK: Langham Global Library, 2015.

———. "Mission to the Indigenous Communities." In *Mission Without Conquest*, Willis Horst et al., 157–66. Carlisle, UK: Langham Global Library, 2015.

Calhoun, Craig, et al. "Introduction." In *Rethinking Secularism*, edited by Craig Calhoun et al., 3–30. Oxford: Oxford University Press, 2011.

Calhoun, John C. *Union and Liberty: Political Philosophy of John C. Calhoun*. Edited by Ross M. Lence. Indianapolis: Liberty Classics, 1992.

Casanova, José. "The Secular, Secularizations, Secularisms." In *Rethinking Secularism*, edited by Craig Calhoun et al., 54–74. Oxford: Oxford University Press, 2011.

Cassaniti, Julia, and Tanya Marie Luhrmann. "Encountering the Supernatural: A Phenomenological Account of Mind." *Religion and Society: Advances in Research* 2 (2011) 37–53.

Cavanaugh, William T. *The Myth of Religious Violence: Secular Ideology and the Roots of Modern Conflict*. Oxford: Oxford University Press, 2009.

Comaroff, Jean, and John L. Comaroff. "Notes on Afro-Modernity and the Neo World Order: An Afterword." In *Producing African Futures: Ritual and Reproduction in a Neoliberal age*, edited by Brad Weiss, 329–47. Leiden: Brill, 2004.

Cotterell, Peter. *Prosperity Theology*. Leicester: Religious and Theological Studies Fellowship, 1993.

Dawkins, Richard. *The God Delusion*. New York: Houghton Mifflin Harcourt, 2006.

Derrida, Jacques. *Specters of Marx: The State of the Debt, the Work of Mourning, and the New International*. New York: Routledge, 1994.

Evans-Pritchard, E. E. "Religion and the Anthropologist." In *Social Anthropology and Other Essays*, 155–71. New York: Free Press, 1964.

———. *Witchcraft, Oracles and Magic Among the Azande*. Oxford: Clarendon, 1937.

Fanon, Frantz. *Black Skin, White Masks*. Translated by Charles Lam Markmann. London: Pluto Press, 1986. Originally published as *Peau Noire, Masques Blancs* (France : Éditions du Seuil, 1952).

Fauconnier, Gilles, and Mark Turner. *The Way We Think: Conceptual Blending and the Mind's Hidden Complexities*. New York: Basic, 2002.

Fish, Stanley. *Is There a Text in This Class? The Authority of Interpretive Communities*. London: Harvard University Press, 1980.

Foxcroft, Gary, and Emilie Secker. "Report on Accusations of Witchcraft Against Children in Akwa Ibom State, Nigeria." Lancaster, UK: Stepping Stones Nigeria, 2010. http://static1.squarespace.com/static/53996fa5e4b0719132a72270/t/54db5f37e4b0d12a4861efd3/1423662903091/Report+on+accusations+of+witchcraft+against+children+in+akwa+ibom+state+nigeria.pdf.

Geertz, Clifford. "Religion As a Cultural System." In *The Interpretation of Cultures: Selected Essays*, edited by Clifford Geertz, 87–125. Illinois: Fontana, 1993.

Gibbs, Raymond W., Jr. "Why Cognitive Linguists should care more about empirical methods." In *The Cognitive Linguistics Reader*, edited by Vyvyan Evans et al., 40–56. London: Equinox, 2007.

Gifford, Paul. *Christianity, Politics and Public Life in Kenya*. London: Hurst, 2009.

Gillespie, John, and Pip Nicholson. *Law and Development and the Global Discourses of Legal Transfers*. Cambridge: Cambridge University Press, 2012.

Goffman, Erving. *Frame Analysis; An Essay on the Organization of Experience*. Boston: Northeastern University Press, 1974.

Goulet, Denis. "Development Experts: The One-Eyed Giants." *World Development* 8 (1980) 481–89.

Greeley, Andrew, and Michael Hout. *The Truth about Conservative Christians: What They Think and What They Believe*. Chicago: University of Chicago Press, 2006.

Green, Edward. *Broken Promises: How the AIDS Establishment Has Betrayed the Developing World*. Sausalito, CA: Poli Point, 2011.

Gupta, Akhil. "Blurred Boundaries: The Discourse of Corruption, the Culture of Politics, and the Imagined State." *American Ethnologist* 22, no.2 (1995) 375–402.

Gupta, Akhil, et al. "State, Corruption, Postcoloniality: A Conversation with Akhil Gupta on the 20th Anniversary of 'Blurred Boundaries.'" *American Ethnologist* 42 (2015) 581–91.

Gutt, Ernst-August. "The So-What Factor and the New Audience." Second keynote paper presented at the Bible Translation Conference, ETP, UK Campus, Horsleys Green, UK, February 5–6, 2008. Accessed July 2, 2011. http://homepage.ntlworld.com/ernst-august.gutt/The%20so-what%20factor%20and%20the%20new%20audience%20pre-pub.pdf /.

Hallowell, A. Irving. "The History of Anthropology as an Anthropological Problem." In *Contributions to Anthropology: Selected Papers of A. Irving Hallowell*, edited by Raymond Fogelson et al., 22. Chicago: University of Chicago Press, 1976.

Halman, Loek. *The European Values Study: A Third Wave*. 2001. http://www.gesis.org/en/services/data-analysis/survey-data/european-values-study/3rd-wave-19992000/.

Harries, Jim. "African Development and Dependency in the Light of Post-Modern Epistemology." *William Carey International Development Journal* 1, no.3 (2012). http://www.wciujournal.org/journal/article/african-development-and-dependency-in-the-light-of-post-modern-epistemology.

———. "African Pentecostalism in Intercultural Linguistic Context." *Journal of the European Pentecostal Theological Association* 33, no.1 (2013) 91–104.

———. "Anti-Racist Strategies in the West Perpetuate Global Poverty: A Critique from Africa." Unpublished. https://www.academia.edu/16703458/When_God_is_Fortune_when_Fortune_is_God_discussing_the_divine_in_Africa_and_the_World.

———. "Building Castles in the Sky: A Case For the Use of Indigenous Languages (and Resources) in Western Mission-Partnerships to Africa." Presented at the Vulnerable Mission Workshop, Pasadena, California, September 24, 2013.

———. *Communication in Mission and Development: Relating to the Church in Africa*. Oregon: Wipf and Stock, 2013.

———. "The Glaring Gap: Linguistics, Anthropology, Religion, and Christianity in African Development." *Exchange: Journal of Missiological and Ecumenical Research* 42, no.3 (2013) 232–51.

Bibliography

———. "The Immorality of Aid to the 'Third World' (Africa)." In *Vulnerable Mission: Insights into Christian Mission to Africa From a Position of Vulnerability*, 23–40. Pasadena: William Carey Library, 2011.

———. "Intercultural Dialogue—an overrated means of acquiring understanding examined in the context of Christian Mission to Africa." *Exchange: Journal of Missiological and Ecumenical Research* 37, no.2 (2008) 174–89.

———. "'Is it Post-Modern, or Is It Just the Real Thing?' Challenging Inter-cultural Mission—A Parable." *Global Missiology* 3, no.8 (2011). Accessed May 10, 2011. http://ojs.globalmissiology.org/index.php/english/article/view/585.

———. "Material Provision or Preaching the Gospel: Reconsidering Holistic (integral) Mission." In *Vulnerable Mission: Insights into Christian Mission to Africa From a Position of Vulnerability*, 81–98. Pasadena: William Carey Library, 2011.

———. "Mission in a Post Modern World: Issues of Language and Dependency in Post-Colonial Africa." *Exchange: Journal of Missiological and Ecumenical Research* 39, no.4 (2010) 309–30.

———. "The Name of God in Africa and Related Contemporary Theological, Development and Linguistic Concerns." In *Vulnerable Mission: Insights into Christian Mission to Africa From a Position of Vulnerability*, 1–22. Pasadena: William Carey Library, 2011.

———. *New Foundations for Appreciating Africa: Beyond Religious and Secular Deceptions*. World of Theology Series 9, World Evangelical Alliance. Bonn: Verlag fuer Kultur und Wissenschaft, 2016.

———. "Pragmatic Theory Applied to Christian Mission in Africa: With Special Reference to Luo Responses to 'bad' in Gem, Kenya." PhD Thesis, University of Birmingham, 2007. Accessed January 2, 2010. http://etheses.bham.ac.uk/15/.

———. "Racism in Reverse: The Impact of the West on Racism in Africa." In *Vulnerable Mission: Insights into Christian Mission to Africa From a Position of Vulnerability*, 163–84. Pasadena: William Carey Library, 2011.

———. *Secularism and Africa: In the Light of the Intercultural Christ*. Eugene, Oregon: Wipf and Stock, 2015.

———. "Sin v. Taboo Compatibility in Africa and the West: Implications for Inter-Cultural Mission, Church, and Majority World Development." *Evangelical Review of Theology* 39, no.2 (2015) 157–69.

———. *Theory to Practice in Vulnerable Mission: An Academic Appraisal*. Oregon: Wipf and Stock, 2012.

———. "When God Is Fortune, When Fortune Is God—Discussing the Divine in Africa and the World." Unpublished.

———. "Witchcraft, Envy, Development, and Christian Mission in Africa." *Missiology: An International Review* 40, no.2 (2012) 129–39.

Healey, Joseph G. *A Fifth Gospel: The Experience of Black Christian Values*. Maryknoll, NY: Orbis, 1981.

Henrich, Joseph, et al. "The Weirdest People in the World?" *Behavioral and Brain Sciences* 33 (2010) 61–135.

Hiebert, Paul. "The Flaw of the Excluded Middle." *Missiology. An International Review* 10, no.1 (1982) 35–47.

Hoehler-Fatton, Cynthia. *Women of Fire and Spirit: History, Faith and Gender in Roho Religion in Western Kenya*. Oxford: Oxford University Press, 1996.

Bibliography

Hof, Eleonora. "Towards a Theology of Vulnerability as Analyzing and Critiquing Strategies of Ignorance and Invulnerability." In *Edward Schillebeeckx and the Theology of Public Life*, edited by Stephan van Erp et al. Publication expected early 2017.

Hoffman, Donald. "Do We See Reality As It Is?" TED Talks. Ted.com. Filmed March 2015. Accessed November 7, 2015. https://www.ted.com/talks/donald_hoffman_do_we_see_reality_as_it_is?language=en.

Hoksbergen, Roland, et al. "International Development: Christian Reflection on Today's Competing Theories." *Christian Scholars Review* 39, no.1 (2009) 11–35.

Horton, Robin. "African Traditional Thought and Western Science." Part I: *Africa* 37, no.1 (1967) 50–71, and Part II: *Africa* 37, no.2 (1967) 155–87.

———. *Patterns of Thought in Africa and the West*. Cambridge: Cambridge University Press, 1993.

Horst, Willis, et al. *Mission without Conquest: An Alternative Missionary Practice*. Carlisle, UK: Langham Global Library, 2015.

Huntington, Samuel P. *The Clash of Civilizations and the Remaking of World Order*. London: Simon and Schuster, 2002.

Ingram, James D. "The Revolutionary Origins of Human Rights: History, Politics, Practice." *Journal for Human Rights / Zeitschrift für Menschenrechte* 9, no.1 (2015) 9–25.

Jenkins, Philip. *The Next Christendom: The Coming of Global Christianity*. Oxford: Oxford University Press, 2002.

Johnson, Thomas K. *The First Step in Missions Training: How Our Neighbors Are Wrestling With God's General Revelation*. Bonn: Verlag fuer Kultur und Wissenschaft, 2014.

Jones, Ben. "The Church in the Village, the Village in the Church: Pentecostalism in Teso, Uganda." *Cahiers d'Études africaines* XLV, no.2 (2005) 497–517.

———. "The Making of Meaning: Churches, Development Projects and Violence in Eastern Uganda." *Journal of Religion in Africa* 43 (2013) 74–95.

Kasomo, Daniel. *The Belief in Mystical Powers in African Traditional Religion: The Meaning, Manifestations, Usefulness and Effects*. Saarbrücken, Germany: Lambert Academic, 2010.

Kanyoro, Musimbi R. A. "The Politics of the English Language in Kenya and Tanzania." In *English Around the World: Sociolinguistic Perspectives*, edited by Jenny Cheshire, 402–19. Cambridge: Cambridge University Press, 1991.

Kaufman, Gordon D. *The Theological Imagination: Constructing the Concept of God*. Philadephia: Westminster, 1981.

Keane, Webb. *Christian Moderns*. Berkeley: University of California Press, 2007.

Lawrence, Peter. *Road Belong Cargo: A Study of the Cargo Movement in the Southern Madang District, New Guinea*. Long Grove, Illinois: Waveland, 1989.

Lewis, C. S. *The Abolition of Man: How Education Develops Man's Sense of Morality*. New York: MacMillan, 1955.

Losurdo, Domenico. *Liberalism: A Counter-History*. Translated by Gregory Elliott. London: Verso, 2011.

Luhrmann, Tanya Marie. "A Hyperreal God and Modern Belief: Toward an Anthropological Theory of Mind." *Current Anthropology* 53, no.4 (2012) 371–95.

———. "Making God Real and Making God Good: Some Mechanisms Through Which Prayer May Contribute to Healing." *Transcultural Psychiatry* 50, no.5 (2013) 707–25.

———. "Symposium Response: Talking to God in Accra." *Pastoral Psychology* 63 (2014) 229–34.

Bibliography

———. "Talking Back about *When God Talks Back*." *HAU: Journal of Ethnographic Theory* 3, no.3 (2013) 389–98.

———. "Toward An Anthropological Theory of Mind." *Suomen Antropologi: Journal of the Finnish Anthropological Society* 36, no.4 (2011) 5–69.

———. "When Demons Are Real." Sunday Review, *New York Times*, December 28, 2013.

———. *When God Talks Back: Understanding the American Evangelical Relationship With God*. Toronto: Random House, 2012.

Luhrmann, Tanya Marie, et al. "The Absorption Hypothesis: Learning to Hear God in Evangelical Christianity." *American Anthropologist* 112, no.1 (2010) 66–78.

Lurhmann, Tanya Marie, et al. "Hearing Voices in Different Cultures: A Social Kindling Hypothesis." *Topics in Cognitive Science* 7, no.4 (2015) 646–63.

Madsen, Richard. "Secularism, Religious Change, and Social Conflict in Asia." In *Rethinking Secularism*, edited by Craig Calhoun et al., 248–69. Oxford: Oxford University Press, 2011.

Magesa, Laurenti. *African Religion: The Moral Traditions of Abundant Life*. Nairobi: Paulines Publications Africa, 1997.

Maier, Gerhard. *The End of the Historical-Critical Method*. St. Louis: Concordia, 1974.

Malo, Shadrack. *Jaluo*. Nairobi: Professor J. O. Malo, 1999.

Manala, Matsobane J. "Witchcraft and Its impact on Black African Christians: A Lacuna in the Ministry of the Hervormde Kerk in Suidelike Afrika." *HTS Theological Studies* 60, no.4 (2004) 1491–1511.

Mangalwadi, Vishal. *The Book That Made Your World: How the Bible Created the Soul of Western Civilization*. Nashville, Tennessee: Thomas Nelson, 2011.

Maranz, David. *African Friends and Money Matters: Observations From Africa*. Dallas: SIL International, 2001.

Marty, Martin E. "Too Bad We're So Relevant: The Fundamentalism Project Projected." *Bulletin of the American Academy of Arts and Sciences* 49, no.6 (1996) 22–38.

Marty, Martin E., and R. Scott Appleby. "Conclusion: An Interim Report on a Hypothetical Family." In *Fundamentalisms Observed. The Fundamentalism Project*, Volume 1, edited by Martin E. Marty and R. Scott Appleby, 814–42. Chicago: University of Chicago Press, 1991.

Marx, Karl, and Friedrich Engels. *Manifesto of the Communist Party*: Chapter 1, 1848. https://www.marxists.org/archive/marx/works/1848/communist-manifesto/ch01.htm.

Masuzawa, Tomoko. *The Invention of World Religions: Or, How European Universalism Was Preserved in the Language of Pluralism*. London: University of Chicago Press, 2005.

Mauss, Marcel. *The Category of the Person*. Cambridge: Cambridge University Press, 1985.

Mazrui, Alamin M. "Language and the Quest for Liberation in Africa: The Legacy of Frantz Fanon." *Third World Quarterly* 14, no.2 (1993) 351–63.

Mboya, Paul. *Luo Kitgi gi Timbegi*. 1997.

———. *Richo ema Kelo Chira*. Nairobi: East African Publishing House, 1978.

McLeod, Saul. "Carl Rogers." 2007. Accessed October 25, 2013. http://www.simplypsychology.org/carl-rogers.html.

Mead, Margaret. *Coming of Age in Samoa*. London: Harper Perennial, 1971.

Meagher, Kate. "Trading on Faith: Religious Movements and Informal Economic Governance in Nigeria." *The Journal of Modern African Studies* 47, no.3 (2009) 397–423.

Bibliography

Mignolo, Walter. "Epistemic Disobedience, Independent Thought and Decolonial Freedom." *Theory, Culture and Society* 26, no.7–8 (2009) 1–23.

Miller, David. *Stuff.* Cambridge, UK: Polity, 2010.

Moyn, Samuel. "Did Christianity Create Liberalism?" *Boston Review*, February 9, 2015. Accessed November 23, 2015. http://bostonreview.net/books-ideas/samuel-moyn-larry-siedentop-christianity-liberalism-history.

Moyo, Dambisa. *Dead Aid: Why Aid Is Not Working and How There Is Another Way for Africa.* London: Allen Lane, Penguin, 2010.

Niehaus, Isak. *Witchcraft and a Life in the New South Africa.* Cambridge: Cambridge University Press, 2013.

Nongbri, Brent. *Before Religion: A History of a Modern Concept.* London: Yale University Press, 2013.

———. "Dislodging 'Embedded' Religion: A Brief Note on a Scholarly Trope." *Numen* 55 (2008) 440–60.

Odaga, Asenath Bole. "Christianity and the African Customary Practices." Maarifa Lecture given at Kima International School of Theology, Kenya, June 23, 2004. Unpublished.

Ogot, Bethwell A. "The Construction of Luo Identity and History." In *Building on the Indigenous: Selected Essays, 1981–1998,* 179–204. Kisumu: Anyange, 1999.

Paul, Frank, and Ute Paul. "Serving as Guest-Missionaries in the Argentine Chaco: Stories of Accompaniment." In *Mission without Conquest: An Alternative Missionary Practice,* Willis Horst et al., 47–53. Carlisle, UK: Langham Global Library, 2015.

Pinker, Steven. *The Blank Slate: The Modern Denial of Human Nature.* London: Penguin, 2002.

Pinker, Steven, and Rebecca Newberger Goldstein. "The Long Reach of Reason." TED talks (animated), filmed February 2012. Accessed November 7, 2015. https://www.ted.com/talks/steven_pinker_and_rebecca_newberger_goldstein_the_long_reach_of_reason?language=en.

Plantinga, Alvin. "Reason and Belief in God." In *Faith and Rationality: Reason and Belief in God,* edited by A. Plantinga and N. Wolterstorff, 16–93. London: University of Notre Dame Press, 1983.

Prah, Kwesi Kwaa. "Introduction: Winning Souls Through the Written Word." In *The Role of Missionaries in the Development of African Languages,* edited by Kwesi Kwaa Prah, 1–34. Cape Town: CASAS, 2009.

———, ed. *The Role of Missionaries in the Development of African Languages.* Cape Town: CASAS, 2009.

Priest, Robert J. "Cultural Anthropology, Sin, and the Missionary." In *God and Culture: Essays in Honor of Carl F.H. Henry,* edited by D. A. Carson and John D. Woodbridge, 85–105. Carlisle: Paternoster, 1993.

Qur'an. *Translation of the Meanings of the Noble Qur'an in the English Language.* Muhammad Taqî-ud-Dîn Al-Hilâlî and Muhammad Muhsin Khân. Madinah, KSA: King Fahd Complex for the Printing of the Holy Qur'an, n.d.

Raringo, Jacktone Keya. *Chike Jaduong e Dalane.* Ugunja, Kenya: Geranya Agencies, n.d.

Reese, Robert. *Roots and Remedies of the Dependency Syndrome in World Missions.* Pasadena: William Carey Library, 2010.

Reitan, Eric. "Moving the Goalposts? The Challenge of Philosophical Engagement with the Public God Debates." *Philo* 13, no.1 (2010) 80–93.

Reynolds, Jack. "Jacques Derrida (1930–2004)." *Internet Encyclopedia of Philosophy,* 2010. Accessed August 30, 2012. www.iep.utm.edu/derrida/.

Bibliography

Richmond, Yale, and Phyllis Gestrin. *Into Africa: A Guide to Sub-Saharan Culture and Diversity*. 2nd ed. London: Intercultural, 2009.

Robbins, Joel, et al. "Evangelical Conversion and the Transformation of the Self in Amazonia and Melanesia: Christianity and the Revival of Anthropological Comparison." *Comparative Studies in Society and History* 56, no.3 (2014) 559–90.

Rori, Andrew, et al. "Revitalizing Youth Entrepreneurship in Kenya: A Deliberate Training Curriculum." *International Journal of Current Research* 3, no.10 (2011), 121–25.

Ross, Steven M, and Gary R. Morrison. "Measurement and Evaluation Approaches in Instructional Design: Historical Roots and Current Perspectives." In *Instructional Design: International Perspectives. Volume 1: Theory, Research and Models*, edited by Robert D. Tennyson et al., 327–54. London: Routledge, 1997.

Rozin, Paul, and Carol Nemeroff. "The Laws of Sympathetic Magic: A Psychological Analysis of Similarity and Contagion." In *Cultural Psychology: Essays on Comparative Human Development*, edited by J. Stigler et al., 205–32. Cambridge: Cambridge University Press, 1990.

Sachs, Jeffrey. "The End of the World as we know it: the fight against extreme poverty can be won, but only if Bush recognises that military might alone won't secure the world." *Guardian*, April 5, 2005. Accessed May 16, 2005. http://www.commondreams.org/views05/0405-26.htm.

Samuel, Vinay, and Chris Sugden. "Mission Agencies as Multinationals." *International Bulletin of Missionary Research* 7, no.4 (1983) 152–55.

Sanneh, Lamin. *Translating the Message: The Missionary Impact on Culture*. New York: Orbis, 1989.

Schirrmacher, Thomas. *Racism. With an Essay by Richard Howell on Caste in India*. Translated by Richard McClary. Bonn: Verlag fuer Kultur und Wissenschaft, 2011.

Senghor, Leopold Sedar. "On Negrohood: Psychology of the African Negro." In *African Philosophy: Selected Readings*, edited by Albert G. Mosley, 116–27. London: Prentice Hall International, 1995.

Shaw, R. Daniel. "Beyond Contextualization: Toward a Twenty-First-Century Model for Enabling Mission." *International Bulletin of Missionary Research* 34, no.4 (2010) 208–15.

Siedentop, Larry. *Inventing the Individual: The Origins of Western Liberalism*. Middlesex: Allen Lane, Penguin, 2014.

Smith, Graeme. *A Short History of Secularism*. London: I.B. Tauris and Co. Ltd., 2008.

Sweetman, Brendan. "The Deconstruction of Western Metaphysics: Derrida and Maritain on Identity." In *Postmodernism and Christian Philosophy*, edited by Roman T. Ciapalo, 230–47. Indiana: American Maritain Association, 1997.

Taylor, Charles. "Western Secularity." In *Rethinking Secularism*, edited by Craig Calhoun et al., 31–53. Oxford: Oxford University Press, 2011.

Thiselton, Anthony C. "Situating a Theoretical Framework: 'Biblical Studies and Theoretical Hermeneutics' (1998)." In *Thiselton on Hermeneutics*, 17–32. Aldershot: Ashgate, 2006.

Tippett, Alan. *The Integrating Gospel and the Christian: Fiji 1835-67*. Pasadena: William Carey Library, 2015.

Tshehla, Samuel M. "Can Anything Good Come Out of Africa? Reflections of a South African Mosotho Reader of the Bible." *Journal of African Christian Thought* 5, no.1 (2002) 15–24.

Venuti, Lawrence. *The Scandals of Translation: Towards an Ethics of Difference*. London: Routledge, 1998.
Ware, Bishop Kallistos. *The Orthodox Way*. Revised ed. New York: St. Vladmir's Seminary, 1995.
Watkins, Mary. *Invisible Guests*. Boston, MA: Sigo, 1986.
Weber, M. *From Max Weber: Essays in Sociology*. Translated and edited by H. H. Gerth and C. Wright Mills. France: Ulan Press, 2012.
Williams, James. *Understanding Poststructuralism*. Abingdon: Routledge, 2014.
Williams, Mallence Bart. "Le Pillage des Ressources Africaines par L'occident." Tedx talk, 2016. https://www.youtube.com/watch?v=t3t3cHb6R34.
Winter, Ralph D. *Frontiers in Mission: Discovering and Surmounting Barriers to the Missio Dei*. Pasadena: William Carey International University Press, 2008.
Winter, Steven L. "Frame Semantics and the 'Internal Point of View.'" In *Law and Language: Current Legal Issues 2011, Volume 15*, edited by Michael Freeman and Fiona Smith, 115–27. Oxford: Oxford University Press, 2013.
Winther, Mats. "The Burning Issue: Race and Racialism." 2015. http://www.two-paths.com/racial_problem.htm.
Wood, Graeme. "What ISIS Really Wants: The Islamic State is no mere collection of psychopaths. It is a religious group with carefully considered beliefs, among them that it is a key agent of the coming apocalypse. Here's what that means for its strategy—and for how to stop it." 2015. http://www.theatlantic.com/magazine/archive/2015/03/what-isis-really-wants/384980/.
Yancey, George. "Recalibrating Academic Bias." *Academic Questions* 25, no.2 (2012) 267–78.
Young, Robert J. C. *Postcolonialism: A Very Short Introduction*. Oxford: Oxford University Press, 2003.

www.ingramcontent.com/pod-product-compliance
Lightning Source LLC
Chambersburg PA
CBHW071454150426

43191CB00008B/1341